Wisconsin Capitol

Fascinating Facts

Wisconsin Capitol
Fascinating Facts

by Diana Cook

PRAIRIE OAK PRESS
Madison, Wisconsin

Prairie Oak Press
2577 University Avenue
Madison, Wisconsin 53705

Typeset by KC Graphics, Inc., Madison, Wisconsin
Printed in the United States of America
by BookCrafters, Chelsea, Michigan

Library of Congress Cataloging-in-Publication Data

Cook, Diana, 1936–
    Wisconsin Capitol: fascinating facts / by Diana Cook.
        p.   cm.
    Includes index.
    ISBN 1-879483-02-5 (pbk.): $9.95
    1. Wisconsin State Capitol (Madison, Wis.) 2. Madison (Wis.)—
—Buildings, structures, etc. I. Title.
F589.M18W573   1991   91-7976
977.5′83—dc20   CIP

Printed on Recyclable Paper

Author's Note

This book is my personal collection of facts, legends, and stories about the Wisconsin State Capitol. It is eclectic in nature and by design, and is not meant to be either a comprehensive history or an inclusive guide. In fact, readers seeking such a book will find it readily in the excellent new edition of the *Wisconsin State Capitol Guide and History*. That book, which I recommend highly, and this one each contain much interesting material not found in the other. They are complementary volumes—both, I hope, of interest and value to all who wish to know more about this most beautiful and significant building.

In compiling this book, I depended greatly on newspaper accounts from the *Wisconsin State Journal,* beginning in 1906, the *Wisconsin Blue Book* in its many editions, and the Capitol Commission General Files in the Archives of the State Historical Society of Wisconsin. In addition, I owe a great debt to the following people who provided information: Dale Dumbleton, Director, Bureau of Building Management–Capitol; Martha Kilgour, granddaughter of Carolyn Howe Porter; Geri Snyder, head of the Capitol Tour Guides; and Michael Stark, Landscape Architect for the Capitol and Executive Residence. I also am grateful to Daniel N. Abrahamson, who read the manuscript and offered valuable suggestions.

Contents

A Monumental Task

The fire whistle—two blasts, then eight blasts, a pause, repeated three times—shattered the silence of the winter night shortly after 3 A.M. on Saturday, February 27, 1904. A night watchman at the Capitol had smelled smoke and discovered a fire in the cloak room in the south wing. Apparently a gas lamp had ignited new varnish on the ceiling.

Although the Capitol had one of the most advanced fire-fighting systems of the day, it was of little use that night. The water tank that fed the sprinkler system had recently been drained for cleaning and was still empty. Madison firefighters arrived on the scene and telegraphed the Milwaukee Fire Department for assistance. About six hours after the fire had started, two engines and two hose carts finally arrived by special train.

Spreading the alarm, university students ran up and down Langdon, State, and Lake streets shouting for help and did much of the work of rescuing books from the law library in the north wing. At first they pitched the books into the snowbanks below, then reorganized into a human conveyor belt and passed great armfuls of soggy books to safety. A newspaper story noted that "several ladies were helping in the work."

Fifteen-year-old Joseph Livermore leaped out of bed, grabbed his vest-pocket Kodak, and ran the two blocks to the Capitol when the fire whistle blasted off in the early hours of February 27, 1904. He took this picture from the steps of a grocery store on Main Street. Later he made and mounted prints, sold them for five cents apiece (his father vetoed the price of ten cents), and made enough money to buy a .22-caliber rifle from Montgomery Ward.

Chief Charles Bernard of the fire department lies at his home, 624 East Gorham Street, in a precarious condition as a result of injuries sustained in this morning's big fire. The slewing of a hosecart threw him from the seat shortly after the first alarm was sounded. The chief was thrown with a terrific force against a huge tree. His right knee was badly injured, but the accident dazed the chief only a few moments. Despite the entreaties of the firemen the chief was persistent, and well in front of his men he led them into the blazing capitol. Not for a moment did he falter and it was not until he fell unconscious, suffocated from smoke on the inside of the capitol, did the seriousness of his condition become known. Dr. D. B. Collins was summoned without delay. The chief was tenderly laid in one of the hosecarts and driven to his home.—Wisconsin State Journal, February 27, 1904.

A heroic Governor "Fighting Bob" La Follette dashed everywhere through the burning building, directing the firemen and the labor force and saving many of the state's records. Though soaked from head to foot from the dripping water, he worked with the firemen until 7:30 P.M., when a doctor took him by the arm and dragged him out of the building. The two went to the executive residence on Langdon street where the governor changed into dry clothing.

The historic building is practically a ruin. Most of the framework is there. The majestic dome still projects into the heavens. Passengers on early trains from the South looking on the skyline of Madison, as the sun burnished the city—a glorious spectacle always—could see no difference. There was the capitol. But to the eye only. The soul had fled. The inside of the building is eaten out by fire. The old Madison capitol is no more.—Wisconsin State Journal, February 27, 1904.

A bleak scene of destruction after the fire.

Another little thing that was missing—besides water for the water tank in the sprinkler system—was fire insurance. As an economy measure, the state had allowed the fire insurance policy on the capitol to lapse the previous year and had established its own insurance fund. The new fund contained about $6,000 at the time of the fire. The damage, however, was estimated at $1 million.

While the fire extinguished one long-running debate—whether to enlarge the existing but inadequate capitol or build a new one—it ignited a new controversy. How much bigger and better should the new capitol be? After considering several proposals, the Capitol Commission, which was in charge of procuring plans for the new building, selected the design prepared by the New York architectural firm of George B. Post & Sons. Probably the most influential architect of his time, Post was now in the twilight of his career and the new capitol would be his last hurrah. In fact, Post would die in 1913, four years before his masterpiece was completed. His two sons, familiar with Post's plans for the Capitol, would see the project through to its finish.

The last legislature preferred to be led by demagogues and politicians rather than by the counsel of the honorable and distinguished men who formed the capitol improvement commission. The invitation to enter the first competition was unsolicited by me; in fact, it was at first declined, but having spent a portion of my youth in Wisconsin and having married there, I felt a special interest in so important a work for your state and was induced to reconsider my first refusal. . . . What strikes me as most extraordinary in the legislature is the paradoxical condition of awarding me the first prize and yet withholding the just results of such an award, namely, the employment as architect of the building.—Cass Gilbert (whose design was rejected as too costly), 1906.

Another question debated at length was whether the new capitol should be made to square with the capitol park or with the points of the compass, as the preceding one had. Finally, the layout of downtown Madison determined how to arrange the building. With diagonal streets running into the points of the square and broad avenues running into the sides, it was decided to align the principal entrances with the broad avenues and align the secondary entrances with the diagonal streets. Grand staircases would lead to the principal floor of the building, which would contain the elective and constitutional offices; the floor above would contain the legislative and judicial offices and the ground floor the minor appointive offices.

The state's limited finances together with the need to house the government while the building was under construction made it necessary to extend construction over a number of years and to build one wing at a time. The first wing, the west wing, was begun in October 1906. The fourth and last wing, the north wing, was finished in 1917. The final cost of $7.25 million included decoration, furniture, grounds, and the separate heat, light, and power plant. To each citizen of Wisconsin, the cost was a mere twenty-five cents per year of construction.

The new building is worthy of its exalted station. In some of its features it is undoubtedly the most beautiful public building in America.—Architectural Record, September 1917.

Lew Porter   Carolyn Porter

Lew Porter of Madison was secretary of the Capitol Commission and the supervising architect throughout the entire period
of construction. He dealt with legislators, painters, sculptors,
and construction workers and was praised as a diligent man
with a meticulous eye for detail. His wife, Carolyn, was the kind
of person who gives books for presents but reads them herself
beforehand. After about eight years of dinner table talk about
the new Capitol, Carolyn decided to put her fertile mind and
her wealth of first-hand information to use. She prepared a
lecture, complete with magic lantern slides, and spoke to many
groups in Madison about the details of the Capitol's construction and artwork. Eventually she took her show on the road
so that people around the state could share Madison's pride in
the glorious new Capitol.

The resources of Wisconsin are so ample, the income of the state so abundant, and the spirit of the people is so high and liberal, that anything less in the character of this chief of all state buildings than should properly belong to it, would result in reproach to them to whom the duty of its provision belongs.— Governor's Message, January 1907.

In 1907 shipments of Bethel White Granite—an unusually white and hard building material, indeed "the whitest granite in the world"—began arriving in Madison from Vermont. The contract specified that granite up to the eye line must be free from any perceptible black spots; above that point "no spot should exceed a ten-cent piece in size." Ordinarily shipments were continuous and arrived every three or four days, but an unprecedented drought in Vermont in 1908, which stalled the water-driven power plant that generated electricity for machinery, and severe cold in 1913 and 1914 made shipments erratic. In 1917 the bond that had been established by quarrying, cutting, finishing, and shipping tons of granite to Wisconsin every few days for ten years moved the manager of the granite company to send Lew Porter a can of maple syrup as a reminder of Vermont's other fine product.

---

*I am delighted to hear that you went to Bethel and saw for yourself the condition of the work. I think the time has come when the commission will have to put the screws on Mr. Bickford or they will never get the capitol completed.—*George B. Post to Lew Porter, August 4, 1913.

George Post chose his building materials with consummate care. Soon trains were delivering tons of marble from all over the world—purple and yellow marble from Italy, green marble from Greece, pink marble from Africa, red marble from Germany—as well as from the states of Maryland, Missouri, New York, Tennessee, and Vermont. Red, green, and gray granite arrived from Wisconsin's Marathon, Marinette, and Waupaca counties. In honor of Wisconsin's large Norwegian population, the King of Norway donated the marble for the sixteen pillars that support the circular gallery on the ground floor of the rotunda. For the last leg of the trip, either a mule-drawn cart or a steam roller hauled marble and granite on wagons from the railroad station to the construction site. Because the final few hundred feet that led to the Capitol were uphill, that last mile could take an hour.

Wing-by-wing construction began in October 1906. The need to house the government during construction and to spread out the building costs meant that one wing was built at a time and then occupied when finished. The west wing was the first to be finished, if not quite in time to properly receive members of the legislature when they convened on January 13, 1909. The first floor was still filled with blocks of polished marble, cement, and debris. A few days earlier, after an inspection tour, the governor had been seen attempting to get cement off his clothing and shoes. On the morning of the 13th, workers were still laying the carpet in the Assembly chamber. But a few minutes after noon, the forty-ninth session of the legislature was called to order.

I hold no brief for the architecture of the [Wisconsin] Capitol. It is a style that won't live, that died, in fact, many years ago. But you can't put that much stone into one pile without creating some dignity and majesty. Anyway, there it is, and we should make the most of it.—Frank Lloyd Wright, 1941.

The east wing and the west wing were completed and construction of the south wing was underway when this photograph was taken in 1911–1912. The north wing of the old capitol remains standing at the right.

Never a reticent lot, legislators became authorities not only on tabling bills but also on building tables and other aspects of design. After the Capitol Commission combed the country for an interesting design for the Senate chamber, and found it in Boston, senators advised the Commission that they would be much happier with individual desks than with the connected desks that the unique circular design called for. Over in the Assembly, it struck someone as somehow unbecoming that the Assembly chamber would have the same type of marble—Tennessee marble—as the restrooms. An upscale Botticino marble from Italy was substituted for the Assembly chamber.

In 1909 a stonecutter died in a spectacular accident as a stone was being placed on the pediment of the west wing. Working overtime on a quiet Sunday afternoon in October, workmen suddenly heard a loud crack and saw three hundred tons of granite begin to fall. One worker leaped through a window into the wing and fell prone on the floor. Two workers on the ground ran to the north side and did not stop until they reached the First National Bank. The stone-setting foreman fell eighty feet from the pediment to his death. It was the second fatality to occur since construction had begun on the new capitol. The previous year a laborer was killed by a cave-in in the construction of the tunnel connecting the Capitol to the heating plant.

Carpenters earned thirty cents an hour. Men who mixed cement—by hand—earned twenty-five cents an hour. The job of water boy paid fifty cents a day. The construction crew included one woman. She had been a housekeeper at the old capitol, but the fire left her without a job, and the death of her husband later that year left her with five small children to support. When Governor La Follette heard of her plight, he

Apparently accustomed to heights, four workmen pose over a section of steel structure for the rotunda in 1910.

arranged a job for her pushing a wheelbarrow at the construction site of the new capitol.

The design of the Capitol included some innovative and notable features:

• A clock system so constructed that 175 clocks ran in unison with one master clock. The twelve-foot-tall master clock on the ground floor contained two bellows that pushed air through pipes leading to all the clocks. One bellows operated the clocks in the east and west wings; the other bellows operated those in the north and south wings. Each minute, air was compressed along through the pipes, causing the hands of all the clocks in the Capitol to "jump" at one-minute intervals.

• Elevator shafts, though elevators were not installed until the 1930s. George Post was one of the first architects to design tall buildings and to use elevators.

• An airplane depicted in a mural in the North Hearing Room.

• Widespread use of natural light to illuminate the building's interior, including an extensive network of openings on the roof that filtered daylight to the decorative ceilings, and translucent glass floor blocks on the second floor to transmit light to lower level corridors.

A power plant was built about a half-mile east of the Capitol on a railway siding between Washington Avenue and Main Street. A tunnel nine feet wide and eight feet high connects the power plant to the north side of the east wing and is still in use today. It contained not only piping and wiring but also freight carts for rolling materials to and from the Capitol.

Shopkeepers on Capitol Square had a front-row seat for the best and longest-running show in town, the construction of a spectacular capitol. One of the highpoints occurred in 1914 when the *Wisconsin* statue was raised to the top of the dome. More than fifty years later a man who had worked in his father's furniture store on Carroll Street recalled the day: "My father sat out in front of our store much of the day watching what was going on, and when the statue was in its proper place at the top he hurriedly came in the store, went into our back room shop, got a big lead pencil, and wrote on the wall above the shop door the date and exact time (hour and minute) when that statue rested in its place."

May [our new Capitol] inspire in the Citizens of this great state a patriotism so earnest and so ardent that until all unclean and unlovely places are wiped out let us not be satisfied with our beautiful new Capitol until we make Wisconsin stand among the States of these United States in the pursuit of Life, Liberty, and Happiness.—Carolyn Porter, Capitol lecture.

Artful Achievements

I think it of vital importance to the result of the work that only the very best men should be retained for the decorative work. If their services can be secured, no matter what the result of the work may be, the Capitol Building will have a status as a work of art, which can be gained in no other way.—George B. Post to Capitol Commission member George H.D. Johnson, July 25, 1911.

The construction of the Capitol turned out to be something of a reunion for artists and architects involved in the World's Columbian Exposition in Chicago in 1893. In selecting artists to decorate the building, George B. Post enlisted some of those whose work at the Exposition proved influential. For example:

Karl Bitter had created the sculpture for the Administration Building at the Exposition; he would do much of the exterior sculpture for the Capitol: the west pediment and the east pediment and the four statuary groups around the dome.

Edwin Blashfield had done murals at the Exposition—after which mural decoration swept the country—and would employ his artistry in the Assembly chamber and on the inner dome.

Kenyon Cox had painted one of the domes in the Liberal Arts building; he would create the four mosaic panels in the rotunda and the three-panel mural in the Senate.

Daniel Chester French had executed the seventy-five-foot statue *The Republic;* he would create the *Wisconsin* statue for the Capitol dome.

Francis Millet, director of decorations and master of ceremonies in 1893, would have painted the Supreme Court murals had he lived.

Jean Pond Miner was artist-in-residence and shared the Wisconsin Pavilion with Helen Farnsworth Mears. The statues they modeled at the Exposition found a permanent home in the Capitol.

Charles Turner had been assistant director of decoration at the Exposition and would execute the murals for the North Hearing Room.

Thanks to the long arm of George B. Post, who himself had designed the largest structure at the Exposition, these artists would again contribute to an ambitious project—this time in Madison.

The Capitol Commission was impressed by the reputation of the man selected to do both the mural in the Assembly and the dome painting. Edwin Blashfield not only was a fine muralist and a man of letters but also could be counted on to finish the job on schedule.

The trains did indeed run on time with Blashfield at the controls, for the Assembly mural was ready when the Assembly convened in the new west wing in January 1909. There had even been time for an exhibit at the Fine Arts Building in New York City. On November 22, 1908, the *New York Herald Tribune* published a letter from fellow artist John LaFarge urging the public to view the painting before it was shipped

Architect George B. Post

to Wisconsin. The painting was well received here also, except for one detail. To Wisconsin eyes, something seemed to be missing. Blashfield was summoned and, for an additional $1,000, he painted out one of the Civil War soldiers and painted a badger where the soldier had been standing. Then the picture was complete.

One reason Blashfield worked so quickly was that the only room light enough and large enough for such huge projects—the Vanderbilt Gallery in the Fine Arts Building in New York City—could be rented only for short periods of time, in the summer. Blashfield gave up his annual trip to Europe and spent the summer of 1912 on the dome painting. Sometimes the room temperature reached 104.

*A very splendid piece of work is being done by Mr. Blashfield
for the dome painting. I am inclined to think that it is not only
the best thing that he has ever done, but that it is as fine, if not
finer, than any decorative painting which has ever yet been produced in this country.*—George B. Post to Lew Porter, August
22, 1912.

The dome painting was finished about a year and a half ahead
of the dome and had to be stored in Madison, waiting to be
put in place. When the time came, it was mounted in sections
on the concave side of a great bowl made of an iron frame rein-
forced with concrete with a facing of plaster of paris. Blashfield
was notified when most but not all of the scaffolding required
for mounting the painting had been removed so that he could
both view the work from the ground floor of the rotunda and
use the scaffolding to make any final alterations. He warned
the Commission not to judge the painting from close up,
reminding them that "behind the scenes of a theater, roses are
big as footballs." If the painting looked right from up close it
would look wrong from below. The viewpoint from the ground
was the essential one.

The size of the dome painting can be appreciated by standing
at the marble railing on the first floor of the rotunda. The
painting is actually the same size as the opening within the railing. Its diameter is thirty-four feet, and the figures are about
thirteen feet high.

The same model is thought to have sat for both the central
figure representing Wisconsin in the dome painting and the
seated figure representing Wisconsin in the Assembly mural.

A kid's-eye view of the rotunda. Visitors are accustomed to stepping around the spread-eagled bodies of children who know that the best way to admire the inner dome and vaulted ceilings of the four wings is to lie down in the middle of the marble floor.

What is the matter with the state of Wisconsin? I haven't received my first payment on the statue for the dome of the Capitol. I don't want to worry you about it, but even sculptors have to have a little money to live on!—Daniel Chester French to George Post, December 12, 1912.

Kenyon Cox's four mosaic panels in the rotunda are the only works in the building that were rendered in place. Others were created elsewhere, then brought to Madison for placement. Cox employed no assistants while he was painting the designs at his New York studio and, like Blashfield, worked every day throughout the summer as long as daylight permitted. Executing the designs with 400,000 tiny pieces of colored glass, in four twelve-by-twenty-four-foot panels, high above the floor of the rotunda, was exacting, nerve-wracking work.

For the three panels in the Senate chamber Cox chose an allegorical "Marriage of the Atlantic and Pacific," to symbolize the opening of the Panama Canal. By August of 1914, however, Cox observed that "present European news gives an ironic aspect to my subject."

The wedding of two oceans made one state senator blush, or rather, he said, caused ladies visiting the room to blush and turn their heads. Because the undraped figures are "in a high degree inappropriate and in bad taste and mar the beauty and impressiveness of the senate chamber," Senator Henry Roethe of Fennimore recommended, in a resolution in 1917, that the artwork be removed and disposed of and the walls restored to their original unadorned condition. The resolution did not pass. The Senator also complained about the ventilation system in the Senate. The air, he said, "puts us into a stupor; that is why we pass so many bad laws here, because we are in a stupor and we don't know what we are doing." Twelve years later ventilation fans were installed above the Senate skylight.

In 1976, when the United States opposed a treaty that ultimately would grant control of the Panama Canal to Panama, nationally syndicated political columnist Garry Wills referred his readers to the Capitol in Madison. "The best way to recreate our brief time of imperial bombast," he wrote, "is to visit the Senate chamber in the Wisconsin State Capitol." Wills went on to describe the Kenyon Cox triptych, which celebrates the opening of the Panama Canal by depicting the marriage of Oceanid (the Pacific) and Neptune (the Atlantic) "under the American shield. In the right panel, Europe brings gifts to the wedding; but Columbia has raised her 'Monroe Doctrine' scepter on that side, guarding the approach. . . . That is the world vision that filled men's dreams early in the century, a vision of America throned triumphant, ruling things for all the rest of the world. . . . The city slickers had put one over on the country. It would be shameful to cling to that kind of deal in this kind of world."

The courtroom of the Wisconsin Supreme Court is highly praised for the harmonious decor of marble and murals. This effect was not achieved effortlessly.

The first massive set of marble panels to be installed proved so disappointing in color that they had to be removed and replaced with another type of marble. Retaining an artist to do the murals presented further problems.

One artist said he would need seven years to finish the work—too much time as far as the Capitol Commission was concerned. Another artist, Francis Millet, went down with the *Titanic* on April 14, 1912. Millet, who had had a colorful life as a drummer in the Civil War and an artist-correspondent for the Russo-Turkish war, was returning to this country to confer with the Capitol Commission when the ship struck an iceberg. The meeting had been postponed until spring because "the affairs of the Academy of Rome," of which Millet was director, "to his great disgust, keep him there much longer than he had anticipated," George Post informed the Commission in

December 1911. To convey the size of the *Titanic*, the *Wisconsin State Journal* said that, if stood on end, the ocean liner would be three times as high as the Capitol dome. An artist's rendering assisted readers in imagining this unlikely situation.

For a time it seemed as if the Supreme Court would have no murals at all. Post had designed the room with panels for decorative paintings, and construction was almost complete when he learned that the justices of the supreme court were intent on having quite a different type of decor, namely, portraits of themselves and their predecessors.

In a masterfully diplomatic letter, Post offered an alternate plan that would make the portraits "a much more important feature of the whole wing" than if hung in the high panels of the courtroom. The plan consisted of creating a veritable "Judges Portrait Gallery" in a vestibule or lobby, something "following the general idea of the greatest portrait gallery in the world, that connecting the Pitti and Uffizi Palaces in Florence, which runs across the Arno." There the portraits "would attract far greater attention and have far greater value than they could possibly have" in the courtroom itself. It would be "one of the show rooms of the Capitol . . . practically a Legal Hall of Fame!" declared Post.

At first the justices weren't buying it, and in an aside to Lew Porter, Post admitted gloomily that it probably was "idle for us to attempt to avoid having the portraits hung in the Supreme Court Room. We think it desirable therefore to dispose of them with such system that they will be as unobjectionable and as unobtrusive as possible." A year later he wrote that "a portion of the Court at least still cling to the idea that the portraits should be hung in that room."

Finally, to Post's great relief, the chief justice approved the plan to hang the pictures in the lobby, asking only that the nameplate at the bottom of the pictures be enlarged from five inches to eight inches. Today twenty portraits of past chief justices hang in the lobby, and twenty portraits of other justices line the corridor outside the justices' chambers. The nameplates on the ornate gold frames measure seven and a quarter inches.

Justice Marshall was possessed of a particularly strong aversion to women employes in the Court, and emphatically expressed to me on more than one occasion his belief that woman's place was in the home, and certainly not in the offices of the Supreme Court. A woman's voice emanating from in or about the offices or corridors of the Court would set his nerves on edge and cause him to call my attention to the sharp and rasping quality of it, when I had to confess I had not noticed it.—Gilson C. Glasier, former secretary to Justice Marshall (whose portrait hangs outside the chambers of Justice Shirley S. Abrahamson), in *Autobiography of Roujet D. Marshall, Justice of the Supreme Court of the State of Wisconsin 1895-1918* (1931).

The fifty-third Secretary of State of the United States appears in one of the murals of the Supreme Court room wearing pale green tights and a mauve t-shirt. He is Christian Herter, who as a teen-ager modeled for his father, Albert Herter, the artist for all four murals in the room. In the picture representing English Law, Christian Herter clutches the collar of a large dog and gazes back toward King John, who is on the verge of signing the Magna Carta. Christian studied fine arts at Harvard before entering politics, and he was governor of Massachusetts when President Eisenhower selected him as Secretary of State.

Thomas Jefferson appears in the Herter mural that depicts the signing of the U.S. Constitution, although Jefferson actually was in Paris at the time as Minister to France. Herter knew his history, but as a member of the romantic-realist school of art he was exercising his privilege of artistic license. Jefferson was so important in American constitutional law that Herter painted him into the scene. The same painting is one of the few to show Benjamin Franklin without his glasses.

In an imposing monument such as your state Capitol I always feel that a sculptor should come in as a musician with his instrument plays with an orchestra. He has to adapt himself to the ensemble, otherwise he ruins the whole.—Karl Bitter to Carolyn Porter, March 23, 1914.

The first exterior pediment to be carved was that for the east wing. It was carved in place, after a few problems were overcome. First, a delay in shipment from the quarry in Vermont prevented the Italian carvers Bitter had hired from starting on time. After the carving was underway, Bitter changed the design and consequently the pediment was not finished by the time winter set in. The carvers demanded that the scaffolding be enclosed and furnished with a stove. Thereafter, the carvings were done in sheds, at first on the Capitol grounds and later at the railroad yards on West Washington, then hoisted into place.

According to George Post's original plan, four tourelles or miniature domes were to decorate the outside dome in the places now occupied by statue groups. The Capitol Commission disliked the tourelle motif and decided to replace them with the statuary after discovering that statues by Bitter could be had for the same price.

All three women artists had Wisconsin ties. Vinnie Ream Hoxie was born in a tiny Wisconsin settlement that later became Madison. She is the only sculptor for whom Abraham Lincoln sat ("for no other purpose than that I was a poor girl," she supposed). For half an hour each day for five months Lincoln posed for her, including the day of the assassination. Her career took Ms. Hoxie a long way, and when she died at age sixty-seven she was buried, in her wedding gown, in Arlington National Cemetery.

Carvers at work on the group that represents "Prosperity and Abundance," which overlooks Wisconsin Avenue.

Helen Farnsworth Mears was born in Oshkosh. As a small child she expressed a talent for art and sculpture by biting cookies and bread into shapes of animals and forming dough into tiny dolls. With her parents' encouragement and without the benefit of formal training, she created a figure that was accepted for the Wisconsin exhibit at the Columbian Exposition. Her *Genius of Wisconsin* stands in the circular room on the first floor at the southeast entrance.

Jean Pond Miner, born in Menasha, was only twenty-eight when she was selected artist-in-residence for the Wisconsin pavilion of the Columbian Exposition. She was still working at her art, drawing in pastels, up to the week of her death in 1967 at the age of 101.

The statue of Hans Christian Heg on the King Street walkway was presented to the state in 1925 by the Norwegian Society of America, which had commissioned the Norwegian-American sculptor Paul Fjelde. Identical statues appear in Norway, where Heg was born, and in Waterford, Wisconsin, where he is buried.

Heg came from Norway at the age of eleven, grew up in Muskego where his father published the first Norwegian newspaper in America, journeyed to California in a covered wagon in search of gold, and became state prison commissioner when he returned to Wisconsin. As the Civil War got underway, Heg recruited men for the famous 15th Regiment. He was killed leading a charge at the battle of Chickamauga in Tennessee.

The names of Wisconsin's seventy-two counties are painted on the ceiling of the main corridors on the ground floor, eighteen in each corridor and in approximate geographic order (northern counties in the north wing, and so forth). Names of county seats appear on the ceilings of the northeast, southeast, northwest, and southwest entrances.

The Capitol is not quite finished. The piece of stone in the lower-right hand corner of the picture was never carved. The window is in the south wing facing Main Street.

The most ornate room in the Capitol would be the governor's reception room. For inspiration, George Post and Elmer Garnsey, the interior decorator, went to Europe to visit historic buildings and collect ideas. The Ducal Palace of Venice seemed to capture what they had in mind, and Hugo Ballin, who had studied art in Florence and Rome, was assigned to replicate the Palace's decorative features in Madison.

After creating allegorical ceilings and historical walls for the governor, Ballin went out to Hollywood to work for Samuel Goldwyn. He created sets for the movie *Baby Mine* and produced several movies of his own: *East Lynne, Pagan Love, Journey's End, Jane Eyre,* and *Vanity Fair.*

The work Ballin did in Madison has had mixed reviews.

A member of the Capitol Commission appealed to George Post:

I desire to call your attention to a matter that I feel is of great importance. It is the decorations in the Executive Chamber. This chamber has heretofore been referred to as the "Throne Room"; it is now the "Chocolate Room." I think that Mr. Garnsey should come here, interview the Executive Committee, and make some arrangements for changing the decorations.

The New York artist and critic Louis Untermeyer raved:

Altogether this room will be one of the most striking things in America; it will take rank with the finest imaginative thought we have ever produced, and in sheer force of color it surpasses them all.

A Madison newspaperman:

It looks more like a Chinese restaurant than a palace.

Carolyn Porter found it a bit much:

The reception room itself is too small to secure the effect which made the original room of the Ducal palace so pleasing. I suspect that we in democratic Wisconsin, much as we appreciate a magnificent reception room, have the feeling that the art of a European palace is not suited to us and to our building. It is un-American.

Forbidden Pleasures

Trips to the upper regions of the dome were once a highlight of the Capitol tour. The serious climbing started from the fourth floor, where visitors began to ascend a series of spiral stairways that twisted through the dusty and dimly lighted space between the outer dome and the inner dome (or coffer dome). Two stairways led to a point immediately below the crown. The top offered a guard rail to clutch, a closeup look at the ceiling mural, and a heart-stopping view of the rotunda floor, two hundred feet straight down.

In 1918, the first year that the Capitol was finished, an estimated 65,000 agile people wound their way to the top. Over the years the number of people who wanted to go to the top grew so large that guards found it difficult to take care of them. Older persons frequently had to stop and catch their breath, holding up the procession. Children raced on ahead, to the alarm of their parents. And some, afraid of heights, froze to the railings and had to be pried loose and helped down.

Beyond the coffer dome, another spiral stairway led to the balcony around the base of the *Wisconsin* statue and a panoramic view of the city, especially awesome in the days before air travel was common.

Trips to the top of the outer dome were discontinued in 1931 and to the inner dome during World War II. Today only inspectors, workers on official business, and an occasional photographer are admitted to the dome. But in warm weather months, the outdoor observation platform that circles the base of the dome on the fourth level is open to the public.

Sure would hold a lot of hay.—Sightseer's comment, 1920.

In 1919 a human fly named Frank J. Kadolph electrified a large crowd by scaling the Capitol all the way to the top of the dome, where he posed triumphantly on the top of the statue's head while waving two American flags. Down below, the crowd cheered and the Mount Horeb band played "On Wisconsin." The occasion was a celebration honoring Wisconsin servicemen and women returning from World War I. The largest electric sign on any public building in the world encircled the dome. It was eight feet high, 308 feet in circumference, and spelled out, in 2,850 red light bulbs, WISCONSIN WELCOMES HER SOLDIERS, SAILORS, MARINES, NURSES.

It was an era noted for its craze of walking over the face of buildings, and Kadolph had planned and practiced his route the previous day: starting from the south wing, he boosted himself up using window frames for support; from the observation platform onward he used ropes to cross the dome; finally he lassoed the statue's arm and climbed the rope to the very top. The flags were inside his shirt.

The date was June 12, 1919 (and the next day was Friday the 13th—Kadolph was daring but he wasn't foolhardy). Two years later he was killed in a fall.

Beginning in about 1937, a huge electric W decorated the dome during football season. It was twelve feet high and thirteen feet wide, and its 250 red light bulbs glowed toward State Street and the university on football weekends. The need for blackouts in World War II put an end to the big W.

Several years earlier, the roar of the crowd and a patriotic occasion inspired another man to conquer the dome—though his trip had a sad ending. The Memorial Day parade of 1911 had just concluded when fifty-nine-year-old Frank E. Smith told his companion that he was going to the top of the Capitol to straighten the American flag, which had become entangled around the pole. (Though the dome of the new Capitol was not finished, a flag had been raised, according to tradition, because the top section was complete.) Men, women, and children lining the streets gazed upward as he scaled the pole and straightened the flag—then watched horrorstricken when he apparently misjudged the distance to the platform below the pole and fell 230 feet to his death.

The challenge of the dome was irresistible to daring young men of the day. On the morning of Smith's accident, Oliver P. Day (whose son is now a Wisconsin Supreme Court justice) succeeded in his attempt to reach the top of the framework in the central portion of the Capitol, unlike his several companions who turned back, feeling not as brave as when they started. Upon his return Oliver Day urged great care: "If you make one misstep, it will be all off."

In 1913, when the framework of the dome was nearly completed, a *Wisconsin State Journal* reporter returned from a trip to the top and described the panoramic view. He had to climb eighteen ladders to get there, but, he wrote,
it was worth all the trouble. The huge pile of masonry and steel seemed almost to sway and vibrate with the wind. To the south could be seen Lake Kegonsa with the rolling country in between. To the north and west Lake Mendota lay stretched out from Merrill Springs to the mouth of the Yahara of Westport, and

the view from the further shore ran for miles until the hills of Mount Horeb cut off the view. Madison lay in each direction from Wingra Park to the ice house in Fair Oaks. A St. Paul train could be seen rapidly steaming south past the fairgrounds until it reached the vicinity of McFarland and was hidden from view.

The dome itself is a wonderful example of the builder's art. The whole inside is filled with a timber scaffolding bolted together in which are used 350,000 feet of lumber representing an outlay of $14,000. Eighteen watchmen's clocks are scattered through the pile and each has to be rung each hour of the 24. This means climbing the whole distance up and down 12 times each day and night for each watchman.

As a protection against fire, a water system has been installed with pipes running to every section of the dome. Every two hours day and night the water is turned on and the framework is thoroughly watered down.

A man named Wallace Jaka regilded the *Wisconsin* statue in 1957. The ascent to the work site each day by elevator, spiral staircase, and rope took about thirty minutes. Once on top, he had only a safety line for protection. (In addition to gilding the statue, he repaired the bulletholes that had mysteriously appeared in the thumb and finger of her right hand and cleaned out a nest of starlings in the fold of her gown.) An experienced steeplejack, Jaka had worked on Big Ben in London, installed a radar screen atop the Empire State Building, and still carried scars from an attack by a woodpecker while gilding the lions atop the Minnesota capitol. A few months after working on *Wisconsin,* however, he died of a broken neck and internal injuries in a fall from a cottonwood tree in his own yard while adjusting a television antenna.

Newspaper editor William T. Evjue often wrote about the beautiful sight that the dome offered for miles around, but it bothered him that the dome could be seen only during daylight hours. Two weeks before Christmas in 1921, he started a drive to illuminate the dome, and soon enough money had been raised to purchase floodlights. The dome glowed for the first time on December 24, 1921.

On election night of 1964, eight University of Wisconsin students committed a capitol offense by attempting to scale the building with climbing gear and ropes. Four of them had made it up one story and were just outside the attorney general's office when they were stopped by police. The other four had not yet got off the ground.

The *Wisconsin* Statue

The female figure on top of the Capitol is named "Wisconsin." (She is often called "Miss Forward" because she appears to symbolize Wisconsin's motto, "Forward," but her correct name is "Wisconsin." A statue officially named "Forward" is located on the North Hamilton walkway between Mifflin and Pinckney streets.) A badger squats on top of her helmet between two cornucopias; an ear of corn lies over each ear; an eagle perches on the orb in her left hand; a W appears on her chest. *Wisconsin* measures 186 inches from base to badger. The outstretched arm measures 65 inches, the hand, 15 inches. Although she's hollow, she weighs about three tons.

Wisconsin was created by a late-blooming artist named Daniel Chester French. French didn't discover his talent until age nineteen, when he carved a frog, wearing clothes, out of a turnip. He progressed to much larger projects, such as the Lincoln statue that gazes into the Reflecting Pool from the Lincoln Memorial in Washington, D.C. The young artist Helen Farnsworth Mears of Oshkosh also submitted a design for the statue, but the Capitol Commission rejected the rather bulky figure she proposed. "Maybe the dame will look like a fairy when she is in the air," wrote a member of the Commission, "but there is nothing to indicate it now." The Capitol Commission considered hiring the sculptor Gutzon Borglum, but he seemed not experienced enough to be trusted with work meant to be viewed from a great distance. In the 1930s, however, he proved worthy of carving the presidents for Mount Rushmore.

French created a half-size model of the statue at Chesterwood, his studio in the Berkshires of western Massachusetts, and a full-size model at his New York studio. The statue was cast in bronze in Brooklyn and sent to Madison by train. A team of eight mules met her at the station and escorted her to the Capitol. A derrick, on hand to lift the slabs of concrete up to the dome, raised *Wisconsin* to her pedestal.

I am glad that you find the design of the Wisconsin State Capitol statue difficult and can best illustrate my reason by telling you a story.

When some years since retained to design a very important building, my client expressed great disappointment when I was so long in getting a satisfactory solution of the problem. I told him that I was very glad, for if any fool could have made the design, he never would have come to me and paid me the price.

Seriously, I do not know any more difficult problem that you can give a sculptor, and I do not know anybody more capable

of a satisfactory solution of the proposition than yourself.—
George B. Post to Daniel Chester French, January 7, 1912.

The *Wisconsin* statue is secured by four large nuts and bolts
that are anchored to the building's superstructure.

Anyone who has had a statue gilded lately is well aware of how
expensive a proposition it is getting to be. But the price of gold
leaf is not the only reason that gilding *Wisconsin* in 1990 cost
far more than it did in 1914. The job entailed not only repair-
ing internal and external wear and tear but also correcting
misguided past attempts at restoration. All previous layers were
removed—including a layer of aluminum paint—to allow the
new gilding better adherence to the original bronze surface.
During the cleaning phase the statue was covered with solvents,
then wrapped in tissue. Over a priming layer of red oxide and
a layer of zinc chromate were applied 12,800 sheets of gold
leaf, each measuring slightly less than three and a half inches
square. Altogether the sheets weighed only ten ounces.

Approaches to gilding *Wisconsin* have changed too. On the
two previous occasions, steeplejacks just threw a rope around
the statue, climbed up, and dangled while they went about their
work. This time gilders stood on $40,000 worth of scaffolding.

The 1990 restoration was a labor-intensive job so thorough
that the seventy-six-year-old statue gained a whole new lease
on life.

---

*It is a chaste, graceful and beautiful figure. I wish, however, that
Mr. French might have spent some time in Wisconsin among
our progressive, intelligent, and enthusiastic citizens who have
the true spirit of our motto. Had he done so there might have*

"Guided by a crew of men who looked like so many scrambling mannikins, the bronze statue was slowly raised to the topmost point of the capitol dome this morning. Before thousands of gaping pedestrians who lined the streets on the four sides of the capitol, the massive figure was hoisted inch by inch to the position it will occupy for many life-times. When it was finally settled on the pedestal, an audible sigh of relief went up from those who watched the delicate operation. The awful possibilities presented to the mind by the imaginary snapping of a cable were relieved by the shout from the capitol dome, 'All set!'"—*Wisconsin State Journal,* July 20, 1914.

been more action in the attitude, the face more eager, and the whole figure more forcibly suggestive of Forward.—Carolyn Porter.

Dome Wars

Until recently the dome of the Capitol was exceeded in size only by St. Peter's Basilica in Rome and St. Paul's Cathedral in London. All three have been eclipsed by a new church in West Africa. The highest (525 feet to the tip of the cross) and widest dome in the world now belongs to the Basilica of Our Lady of Peace, in the small city of Yamoussoukro, in central Ivory Coast. This largest church ever built has seating for 7,000 people and standing room for another 11,000. It was completed in 1990 in time for a visit by Pope John Paul II.

Wisconsin has more cows than any other state. According to the State Department of Agriculture, 53 percent of the gross income of $325,000,000 from Wisconsin farms in 1923 was from the milk these cows produced—10 billion pounds—enough to fill the state capitol from the basement to the top of the dome 21 times.—Wisconsin Blue Book, 1925.

It's hard to say which state can claim the tallest capitol because no one measures in quite the same way. Where is the baseline? And where is the top? At the top of the flagpole? The top of the statue? The crown of the dome? Confusion reigns. According to official state guide books, finalists in the U.S. Championship of Domes—flagpoles, statues, and all—would include Illinois, 405 feet; Texas, 309 feet; Kansas, 304 feet; West Virginia, 293 feet; Washington State, 287 feet. The official height of Wisconsin's Capitol is 285.9 feet, a respectful nineteen inches shorter than the Capitol in Washington, D.C. The *Freedom Triumphant* statue on Washington's dome, however, is four feet taller than *Wisconsin* on Wisconsin's.

Both the Wisconsin and the U.S. capitols have double domes; the inner dome and the outer dome are separate. In Washington both domes are made of cast iron, and the outer one has been painted white to match the marble of the rest of the building. The Wisconsin outer dome is made of the same white Vermont granite as the rest of the exterior and rests on 2,500 tons of steel. Wisconsin's is the only granite dome in the United States.

For several weeks in 1914, two stories shared the front page of the *Wisconsin State Journal:* the assassination of Archduke Ferdinand and the approach of World War I, and the question of which direction the *Wisconsin* statue should face. Newspaper readers responded to the latter issue by the hundreds and with passion—

The East, whence comes the rising sun and the new day, typifies all the hopes of the human race from its inception to the end of time. He who looks not forward to the new day from each setting sun lives without a future and without a hope. . . . To suggest that it should have its back toward the new day and its face to the west is unthinkable.

poetry—
If my opinion you would ask
I'd say there's only one way.
Face to the undeveloped North
Without any further delay.

more poetry—
Point west! Point west!
That is the way the men were facing
Those who first came hither, lone trails tracing
Point west! Point west!

some cynicism—
The majority of this city would vote to have it face toward
some brewery

and impudence—
Why not place the figure on its back, looking and pointing
upward, the direction in which all of us want to go by and by?

In the end, the Capitol Commission agreed with the citizen
who said that such ornaments generally face the same direction as the main entrance and that the main entrance to the
Capitol must be the one facing the broad plaza leading to the
city's waterfront, the obvious gateway to the city.

The architect and the sculptor had spoken along the same
lines. George Post considered the principal front of the building
to face Lake Monona, and Daniel French felt that the statue
would receive the most favorable light and shade if it faced
southeast.

It all seemed to make sense to the Capitol Commission, which
announced that *Wisconsin* would face toward Monona Avenue
(now named Martin Luther King Jr. Boulevard) and that
entrance would be recognized as the formal entrance to the
building.

People who look for trouble usually find it. Here workers go far out of their way to tuck-point—or seal spaces between the stone blocks—to fight water damage to the dome.

The Great Outdoors

A frozen wasteland by winter, Capitol Park is a spectacle of color from spring through fall. The show begins in May as 46,000 tulips start to bloom, most of them in the circular beds at each corner. When the curtain comes down on the tulips, the bulbs are dug up, put in plastic bags, and sold to the public for two dollars a dozen. The money collected pays for the following year's 46,000 bulbs. The tulip beds are financially self-sustaining, as is Operation Chrysanthemum in the fall.

In the 1950s when the tulips (a mere 6,400 tulips) finished blooming in the four circular beds, the 900 cannas that replaced them were rentals from a commercial greenhouse. At the end of the canna season, the plants went back to their owners. Having no greenhouse and claiming no special expertise in the gardening department, the Capitol grounds crew kept it simple—tulips in the spring, cannas in the summer. Today the summer plantings offer great variety and exciting colors: Gin Pink begonia, Bandit Pink and Ringo White geranium, Yellow Boy marigolds, Rose Pink hibiscus, Chinese Coral canna, Vodka Red begonia, Silver Dust senecio, Firecracker Rose salvia,

Purple Ruffles basil, and many, many more. The grounds crew grows about 20,000 of the plants in greenhouses and purchases others.

The biggest problem is that there's no back yard, no place to throw things and let them sit. You can't hide anything!—Michael Stark, landscape architect, Wisconsin Capitol.

More than half a million people visit Capitol Park annually— 15,000 to 20,000 each Saturday from May to November for the Farmers Market; 20,000 for each of the summer evening Concerts on the Square (a recently revived custom of the 1850s); and as many as 200,000 for Art Fair on the Square in July.

Because the Capitol is a public site, keeping the grounds looking elegant presents a challenge for the grounds crew, their supervisor, and the landscape architect. They are assisted at times by horticulture students and trusted inmates from a correctional institution. They approach the task by dividing the grounds into four equal quadrants so that each of the four groundskeepers has his or her own turf and complete creative and caretaking responsibility for one quadrant. In 1982 the Professional Grounds Management Society recognized their efforts by awarding Wisconsin's Capitol the grand prize.

Chocoholics swoon as they inhale Capitol Park in the springtime after tons of cocoa bean hulls have been spread over the flowerbeds as mulch. The hulls, which preserve moisture and eliminate weed problems, are purchased directly from the Ambrosia Chocolate Company in Milwaukee. Rice hulls from Louisiana are also used as mulch.

Musicians often perform in Capitol Park for special events.

The gold star bed, on Mifflin Street north of Wisconsin Avenue, was originated by "gold star mothers," women who had lost sons in World War I. The mothers who used to admire it from the upstairs tea room of Manchester's department store, formerly across the street, would appreciate it even more today. About 12,000 tiny but intense grape hyacinths and 2,000 tulips make the bed twice its original size.

Many trees in Capitol Park have exotic names but are indigenous to Wisconsin. Details of several trees follow:
• The bur oak at the corner of Pinckney and North Hamilton streets is more than 200 years old.
• The Bauman horsechestnut, at West Washington Avenue, has clusters of flowers resembling popcorn when it blooms in May.
• The katsura tree, at the corner of King and Main streets, is native to China and has heart-shaped leaves.
• The black tupelo, directly off the King Street walkway, has yellow, orange, scarlet, and purple leaves in the fall.
• The red oak tree at the corner of Main Street and Martin Luther King Jr. Boulevard honors the request of a Madison woman that after her death a tree be planted in her memory on the Capitol grounds.

It may appear that the Norway maples on the perimeter of the Capitol grounds are choked by asphalt, but the material that surrounds them is epoxy bonded rock, a special material porous enough to admit oxygen and moisture. It can be trimmed back to allow the trees to grow and is preferable to grass in areas that sustain such heavy foot traffic as the Saturday morning Farmers Market.

I have seen better looking pasture for cattle than the lawn of the State Capitol. Why are people permitted to walk and sit all over the grass? . . . People run their bikes on the grass, play frisbee, walk dogs, and lie all around the park. It looks like a public beach instead of a Capitol Park. What must our tourists think? If nothing else, make more sidewalks where the parks are or put a wrought iron fence around the grounds.—Letter to the Editor, *Capital Times,* May 1980.

"One thing I'm very proud of," says the Capitol's landscape architect, "is that you'll see no Keep Off the Grass signs. It's our belief that the grounds are owned by the people of the state for their use and enjoyment." While people are always welcome to rest, relax, play, and picnic on the grass, he discourages the practice of taking shortcuts across the lawn. Several years ago he solved the cattle path problem with flowers—ten-foot-wide flowerbeds along the walkway—instead of fences. Ever since,

The grounds crew says it with flowers.

people have been sitting on the lawn or sitting along the walkway but rarely are they in such a hurry to get in or out of the Capitol that they clomp through a bed of pink impatiens.

The flowerbed that faces Carroll Street, between West Washington and Main, is the billboard flowerbed. The side of the mounded flowerbed that faces the Capitol changes from year to year—*Badgers,* it may read, or *America's Dairyland.* The side that faces the street is usually sculpted in the shape of the state of Wisconsin. In 1984 a vigilant senator noticed that Washington Island and Door County appeared to be a solid chunk of land. With a shovel and permission, the senator from that district remapped enough alternanthera plants to separate the island from the mainland.

Responding nobly to Uncle Sam's appeal for vegetable gardens during World War I, the Capitol grounds crew planted beans, beets, carrots, and corn around the borders of the flowerbeds in 1918. At the end of the season, their crop was sold for a profit of $25, which was turned over to the Red Cross.

MICHAEL FELDMAN: *We have a capitol right in the middle of our city and it totally confused a visitor from Minnesota. You're confused by what?*

VISITOR: *I was confused by the Capitol. No matter if you're on East Washington or West Washington, if you're going into the Capitol it looks the same. To me that was confusing because I was going into the Capitol and I thought, yeah, that's the same side we went into before, but we had to drive around it a couple times to make sure. My wife said it's not confusing because the statue on top faces only one way but I don't look at the statue when I'm driving.*

FELDMAN: *Unless you have a sunroof or something. How long did you circle the Capitol?*

VISITOR: *It was a while. We're here though.*

FELDMAN: *We get a kick out of it. Mostly it's people from Iowa, just circling endlessly. You're from Minnesota. You don't fit the stereotype. But it's perfectly symmetrical so you could be anywhere.*

VISITOR: *It's a landmark and it's in the middle of town but you can't tell what side of town you're on when you're looking at it.*

FELDMAN: *I don't think you're even here, to tell you the truth. I think you're still missing. I'm glad you found it eventually. Did you just take a turn? They don't let you turn off it either. That's the other thing. You're just whipping around it like a centrifuge. You start going faster and faster, and you see this dome spinning. Actually that's pretty much the Madison experience.*

Whad'Ya Know? Wisconsin Public Radio

Bob Bender and his pristine 1956 Cadillac, which he called Nellie, were stationed at the taxi stand across from Inn on the Park. Over the years they transported many visiting celebrities, including several U.S. Presidents. On the day Nellie's odometer read 999,999, Bender drove the governor of Wisconsin and the mayor of Madison around Capitol Square so that they could witness the momentous appearance of the new zero reading. By the end of 1987, the odometer registered more than 1,032,000 miles—much to the interest of the Guinness Book of World Records. When Bender died at the age of 88 in 1988, Nellie was in the funeral procession.

This Old Capitol

Preservationists are very high-minded people. They aim for purity and fidelity and perfect accuracy. If they find a sock under Mark Twain's bed, they make sure that it is one of Mark Twain's socks and then they don't launder it, they put it back just where he dropped it. If they look in Mark Twain's refrigerator and find a six-pack of Budweiser, they take that out and put in an 1889 lager. It's flat but it's authentic. And this is a great work that they do. They try to stop time so that we can be inside the past, inside a house that looks as much as possible as it did one hundred years ago.—Garrison Keillor, *American Radio Company.*

The Capitol held up quite well under its first sixty years of use, but by 1980 some serious shortcomings had become apparent. The building demanded attention, primarily because of changing space needs, modern office equipment, and piecemeal and inconsistent remodeling. Furthermore, the Capitol as originally designed could not accommodate the growing number of employees. The people in charge of its care faced a decision: which would prevail, the original design or the functions to be housed? Charged with developing guidelines for restoration of the Capitol, the caretakers gave preference to design, yet restoration would proceed with an effort to balance historical identity on the one hand with modern requirements on the other.

Certain "esthetically inappropriate" modifications of past years would have to be corrected. In other words, the tacky fake-wood partitions that created mazes of once-spacious offices had to go. So did the phony acoustical ceilings and the gruesome fluorescent light fixtures. Brass plates would replace plastic plates behind electric switches and outlets. All exposed woodwork would be stripped of paint and varnish down to the bare wood and refinished with just one layer of a natural stain-sealer. The list of "design conflicts" went on.

It was going to be one Rainy Year Project after another until the year 2000. But when the work was finished, the Capitol would be not only restored to its original level of elegance but technologically ready for the Twenty-first Century.

One of the first major restoration projects took place in the Assembly chamber. There an architectural team probed the designs and artwork with scalpels and microscopes to discover the original colors and stencil patterns. At the same time that artists were restoring the past, technicians were modernizing the facilities with more than five miles of new wire and cable to accommodate the latest telephone, sound, and electronic voting equipment. Meanwhile, the ninety-nine members of the Assembly continued their work from metal folding chairs in makeshift quarters throughout the building, responding to roll call with raised hands instead of pushbuttons. By the time the restoration of the Assembly chamber was finished, sixty-five craftsmen from fifteen different trades had contributed to the project.

The *Forward* statue waves goodbye to her friends at the Capitol before being transferred from the North Hamilton walkway to a warehouse for cleaning. The Hans Heg statue on the King Street walkway was enclosed in plastic-wrapped scaffolding and cleaned in place. Ground walnut shells were used in the process of cleaning both statues. The ground shells help to remove dirt and corrosion yet do not damage the surface.

The world's first electric voting machine was installed in the Assembly in 1917, enabling members to cast ballots from their desks by flipping a switch. Formerly, a roll call vote took about twelve minutes; with the new invention it took about one minute. Today's electronic vote takes about eleven seconds.

Cleaning the main mural in the Assembly became known as "Art by the Acre." To work solvents over every inch of the state's largest oil painting—nearly 90,000 square inches—and the smaller murals in the Assembly required eight weeks' time and 20,000 Q-tips. An enzyme system was used to remove the years of dirt and cigar smoke, as well as a layer of polyurethane from the 1960s that had darkened the painting. Cracks caused by shifts in the wall also were repaired. With the aid of infrared photography, eight areas of pentimenti—designs originally painted by the artist but for one reason or another painted over—were identified.

The circular arrangement of thirty-two lights in the dome area of the Assembly chamber is called "ring of pearls," and it takes two people to change a bulb: one to go up to the attic and lower the fixture, and the other to wait forty feet below to replace the bulb when it comes down. The ring of pearls had been removed in the 1960s, possibly after bulb-changers had thrown up their hands in despair, and was reinstalled in 1988 when the new method of lowering the lights with cables was devised.

Artifacts uncovered during renovation of the Assembly offered insights into construction workers' and legislators' habits: a smoking pipe filled with unburned tobacco, the sports page from the August 22, 1908, edition of the *Milwaukee Sentinel,* snuff boxes. Renovation of the north wing also yielded an interesting and significant find. Under three feet of rubble was uncovered an eighty-year-old plaster bust of a young bearded man that had been used as a model for one of the exterior sculptures.

As Wisconsin's major architectural gem, the Capitol is a tribute to the spirit of the people and culture who had it built. It is our continuing task to preserve this magnificent building as a reminder of the past and as a commitment to our future.— Charles Quagliana, Preservation Architect.

The governor's office was restored to its turn-of-the-century look during the first phase of the Capitol restoration. Once again it contains the original mahogany roll-top desk, ten brass wall sconces, and one of the original Capitol clocks, as well as a leather-covered sofa and other furniture. A large chandelier hangs over a four-by-ten-foot worktable. To complete the effect, interior decorators selected a new carpet with a maroon-brown and beige checked pattern and a solid maroon-brown border; mini-blinds and taupe-colored draperies trimmed in dark rose; off-white walls with gold leafing near the upper ceiling; and for the curved ceiling cornices, shades of grey, brown, and taupe to blend with the South American mahogany wainscoting.

An ornamental plaster craftsman, who had worked on the previous interior restorations, gave up his annual job as Santa

Claus to undertake the plaster work required in the restoration of the Executive office.

The French walnut table in the center of the governor's conference room is considered to be the single most important piece of furniture in the state, in view of the number of historic bills that have been signed there. In 1989 the Wisconsin Fraternal Congress picked up the bill—$3,595—for the restoration of the table.

A doorknob that had been in use in the governor's office since 1917 traveled nearly three million miles in space in 1985. When astronaut Daniel C. Brandenstein, whose hometown is Watertown, was a crew member aboard the shuttle *Discovery,* the governor sent along the doorknob, as something unique and of a permanent nature to represent the state.

The only true fireplace in the Capitol is in the governor's reception room. It vents to a chimney and looking up you can see daylight. Apparently it's never been used and had better not be because it is so shallow. The fireplaces in the Senate and Assembly parlors are fakes.

In a short time the entire structure will be restored to its original beauty plus the addition of such modern devices as fluorescent lighting, which was not in existence at the time of the building's construction.—Governor Warren Knowles, Dedication of the Capitol, July 7, 1965.

It is likely that never before have so many extremely large windows been pried out of a building, shipped off to the nearest big city for repair and weatherstripping, then put back in place. In the first phase of the project, 571 windows from the ground floor through the fourth floor were restored in that way. When the project is complete, all the windows above the fourth floor will have had the same treatment. One early proposal would have replaced the twelve-foot-high black cherry windows, which had rotted and leaked air, with $1.7 million worth of aluminum frame units with fake plastic dividers. Aghast at the prospect of the-Capitol-as-ice-cream-parlor, preservationists proved that the decision to restore rather than replace would be less expensive as well as historically correct. A supportive Wisconsin resident even donated his stack of seasoned cherrywood to the cause.

The Capitol has two water systems. Originally untreated water from Lake Monona was used for restrooms, the grounds, and fire protection; a well more than a thousand feet deep, drilled possibly as early as 1850, supplied drinking water. Lake Monona is still the source of water for the grounds; the rest comes from the Madison water utility.

Remove grand stairway and set aside, the work order may well have read. In the 1980s, all four sets of exterior monumental stairs were completely dismantled, in order to replace the deteriorating mortar with modern material. The huge concrete blocks and ballusters that make up each massive stairway were labeled and stacked in their respective driveways, then the pieces of the gigantic puzzle were reassembled and secured with new adhesive.

Since I moved to Madison five months ago, I've been using the Capitol as a compass. . . . I get lost a lot, and when I do, I look around for the Capitol Dome to regain my bearings. As I've begun to meet people, I've learned that everybody's keeping an eye on the Capitol, no matter how long they've lived here or how well they know their way around. For them, the Capitol seems more a spiritual compass, a touchstone, a beautiful reminder of the days when architecture was Architecture. Urbanologist Jane Jacobs has called buildings like the Capitol "frosted pastries on trays," and yet we're all a sucker for these wedding-cake monuments to the past. They feel right in a way that glass-box skyscrapers never do.—Kent Williams, *Isthmus,* June 23, 1989.

The symmetrical design of the Capitol makes it easy to get lost. Governor Gaylord Nelson once said that if the newsstand on the first floor (it's no longer there) were moved to a new location in the middle of the night nobody would be able to find their office the next morning. Newcomers to the building find the attendant at the information counter on the ground floor always helpful in providing directions. In addition, white globes over each exit on the ground floor tell which street lies beyond.

A Madison man who liked to visit his father at the Capitol every day after school in the 1920s recalls that he blazed the trail by lobbing a mud ball onto an overhead light fixture. The maintenance staff didn't notice, probably because bulbs burned out infrequently in the days of direct current (before alternating current), and the mud stuck there for months, fixing the way to Father's office in the Department of Public Instruction in the north wing.

When the Capitol's old steel cage elevators were replaced in the 1950s, the metal latticework found a new home across the street at the Signature Room at the Inn on the Park. At the Badger Candy Kitchen on Main Street, chocolates are prepared on two marble slabs intended for use in the Capitol. The slabs were rejected and offered free to anyone who would haul them away.

In 1913 Lew Porter appealed to George Post to incorporate something into the design that would designate the different wings. By then the wings and the rotunda were starting to connect and already people were confused—"The same thing was true in the old Capitol," he wrote. After considering the matter, Post proposed applying inscriptions designating "North Gallery" or "South Gallery" way up in the frieze at the second floor level—raised bronze letters in classic design, of course. "We do not think it would be wise to have the inscription 'North Wing' and 'South Wing' appear, especially as it is very difficult to find a place where such an inscription would be appropriate."

A few years ago the Capitol's landscape architect offered an artistic solution to the orientation problem. On the southeast lawn he created a large and colorful compass with flowers and plants, in sympathetic acknowledgment of the confusion created by the layout of Madison streets around the Capitol.

In the early 1960s rumors circulated that the Capitol was tilting to the south, as much as fifteen degrees. The state chief engineer investigated and determined that the Capitol was not tilting but the walkway to the south wing was sagging. Inadequate landfill—sawdust, scrap lumber, cans, bottles, and other debris—were replaced with earth fill and new sidewalks were laid.

The Capitol had its first bath in 1965. It took twenty men (firmly anchored to the building) with high pressure hoses ten weeks to administer the steam, water, and chemical cleaning process. Much of the dirt and grime collected over the half century was soot from old coal-burning stoves used in

buildings around the Square for many years. Because the chemicals were harmful to glass and paint finish, office windows had to be covered and parking places sacrificed.

The only original carpeting that remains in the Capitol is in the Supreme Court room.

The United States flag and the Wisconsin flag are flown over the south wing of the Capitol when the Senate is in session and over the west wing when the Assembly is in session. Legislative messengers raise the flags shortly before each day's session begins and lower them as soon as the lawmakers in each house adjourn for the day (or night). The route to the flagpole requires climbing a ladder above the elevator shaft, then a short flight of stairs outdoors. Flags fly over the east wing twenty-four hours a day every day. Flags fly over the north wing only on inauguration day, national holidays, or at the direction of the President.

Until 1973, the Capitol was open to the public only Monday through Friday. Now it is open every day of the year from 6 A.M. to 8 P.M.

The Capitol doesn't have a front door, although Architect George Post felt that the principal front of the building was toward Lake Monona and referred to the boulevard leading to the lake as being in front of the Capitol. He considered the formal approaches to the Capitol to be through the pavilions at the top of the exterior grand staircases rather than through the ends of the wings. Since the entrance at the end of Martin Luther King Jr. Boulevard is the closest the Capitol comes to having a front door, that is where presidential candidates, kings, and other such distinguished guests usually enter when visiting the Capitol.

In the absence of a front door, the Capitol also has no street address. Mail addressed to an office in the Capitol may use a post office box or specify room number and wing (east, west, north, and south) and the zip code 53702.

A state law protects the view of the Capitol. No building constructed within one mile of the Capitol may exceed the height of the columns beneath the base of the dome, or 182 feet above Lake Monona.

Now You Know

Recently I was curious as to the exact orientation of true north at the state Capitol.

I could not find definite information, so I tried to find the answer by observations of the North Star (Polaris) and by means of the sun. Both methods agreed quite closely.

This is what I found: A true north-south line projected through the center of the south edge of the bronze base of the "Forward" sculpture (north of the Capitol) intersects the top step of the approachway, 227.3 feet away, about 53.5 inches east of the building center.

The center of the base of the sculpture appears to be about 4 inches east of building center, so this indicates an angle of approximately 1.04 degrees east from true north for the orien-

tation of the Capitol, accurate perhaps to a 20th of a degree (plus or minus 0.05 degree).

My primary tools for star observations were a plumb line located near the north door of the Capitol and a small light located on the Forward sculpture base.

—John E. Gangstad, Madison, *Wisconsin State Journal,* June 23, 1984.

"Wisconsin's beautiful $8,000,000 capitol building was in ruins today, following a series of mysterious explosions which blasted the majestic dome from its base and sent it crashing through the roof of the east wing," said the *Capital Times* in a story that accompanied this picture on April 1 (April Fool!), 1933. On April 1, 1991, Wisconsin Public Radio reported that Wisconsin legislators had voted to move the capital to the village of Redgranite, seventy miles north of Madison. Only two listeners called in to object to the move.

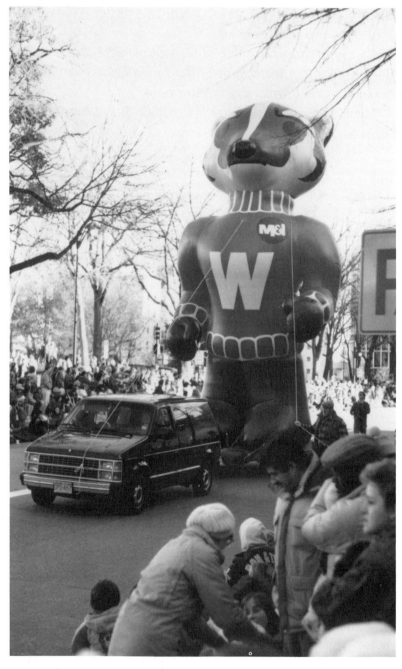

Thousands attend the annual Holiday Parade around Capitol Square in November.

Festivities and Formalities

Francis Ford Coppola, director of the *Godfather* movies and *Apocalypse Now,* staged an extravaganza at the Capitol in March 1980. American flags festooned the State Street entrance, helicopters hovered overhead, and spotlights pointed to the skies. The occasion was the filming of a political commercial for Governor Jerry Brown of California, who was seeking the Democratic presidential nomination. Mr. Brown delivered a thirty-minute campaign speech while a crowd of about 3,000 watched the live commercial on a two-ton television screen affixed to the Capitol.

An event of an equinox festival in 1981 attempted to turn the Capitol into a geometrically tuned instrument sending forth human and planetary energies in a message of world peace. During each of the six hours of winter solstice, beginning at 4:51 P.M., taped and live voices in the rotunda sang a syllable of the word *oceans*—OOOOOO (self), SHHHHH (family), EEEEEE (community). But before they could get to AAAAAA (country), NNNNNN (world), and ZZZZZZ (cosmos), the building was closed, as usual, at 8 P.M. and everyone was asked to leave.

By the time the Capitol was finally finished in 1917, World War I was underway and people were too preoccupied with events abroad to celebrate a building. World War II had also come and gone before the Capitol at last was officially dedicated on July 7, 1965. Outside a pristine Capitol, its exterior having just been cleaned for the first time, about 150 people looked on as the 32nd Division Army band played, 100 color guards massed in salute, and representatives of 30 veterans organizations displayed flags. In the background Wisconsin Young Americans for Freedom marched with picket signs protesting a bill scheduled for consideration, and on the podium the governor gave a belated dedication speech. A walnut box that had once belonged to Governor Dodge was filled with mementos and turned over to the State Historical Society for safekeeping.

The Capitol was rededicated on September 17, 1987, the 200th anniversary of the signing of the United States Constitution.

Wisconsin's centennial celebration of statehood served also as a postwar celebration. On January 5, 1948, for the first time since 1938, thousands of citizens jammed the Capitol. The day began with a parade around Capitol Square led by the Menominee Indian band. Singing and square dancing followed indoors, and that night Governor and Mrs. Oscar Rennebohm led the grand march at the centennial ball.

For years the University of Wisconsin Prom, considered to be the most brilliant social event of the year, was held in the Capitol. Ushers in evening clothes greeted the couples as their cars and carriages arrived at the Monona Avenue pavilion. After the formality of the receiving line in the executive wing,

The opening ceremonies of Wisconsin's Centennial celebration in 1948 included music by the Menominee Indian Band, shown here with Mrs. Oscar Rennebohm, wife of the Governor.

the prom chairman and prom queen led the grand march through the corridors and up and down the grand staircases. A big city orchestra played in the rotunda, a smaller orchestra in the Assembly chamber, and banjo or ukelele music for dining. Dinner was served in the Capitol Cafe throughout the evening, and dancing continued until 3 or 4 A.M.

In 1925 the senate passed an "anti-dancing" bill amid charges that the Prom was getting too rowdy. One irate senator claimed that at the most recent Prom the firehose had been turned on, a large number of students were intoxicated, and a young woman was found lying in a fireplace. The Assembly killed the bill and the Prom continued to be held in the Capitol until 1929, when the new Memorial Union on the campus became the site of the Prom. Only once again, for the sake of tradition in

Orderliness and sobriety prevailed through the seven hours in which joy reigned in the statehouse, according to newspaper coverage the next day. Seven Wisconsin Prohibition agents, a full corps of Capitol police, and a platoon of

officers assigned to special duty found little to occupy them. The Junior Prom,
Class of 1925, took place on February 8, 1924.

Wisconsin's centennial year of 1948, was the Capitol profusely decorated with garlands of smilax and fresh flowers for the Prom. That night 2,000 couples danced to the music of the Lawrence Welk Orchestra and the tune most often requested, "How Soon?"

Prom-goers with their low-cut dresses and silk hats, and coming home neck and neck with the milkman, received a thorough verbal drubbing from W. L. Ames, former president, Farmers National Congress, at last night's meeting of Farmers' Week. "A large gathering at the capitol, where borrowed dress suits, high hats, cabs, flowers, and banquets regale is competing with this session tonight," said Mr. Ames. "Years ago there was an occasional lunatic. Now the world is dance crazy." —Wisconsin State Journal, February 10, 1917.

The Capitol Cafe, which existed in the basement in the 1920s, offered live music and formal dining. Madison society dined on one-dollar steak or fried chicken Sunday dinners, and frequently were joined by such celebrities as Harry Houdini and his wife, Blossom Sealy, and Sophie Tucker.

Inauguration of the governor takes place on the first Monday in January following election. In 1979 the Milwaukee Symphony Orchestra played for the inauguration of Governor Lee Dreyfus. The minister who gave the benediction had also officiated at the governor's baptism and wedding.

The driver of this pickup truck never fully explained what moved him to roar partway up the steps of the east wing, where the truck stalled among billowing smoke from its spinning wheels.

*More than 30,000 people went through the state capitol building
in July, August, and September of this year. . . . The unanimous
opinion of the sight-seers is that the capitol is the finest in the
union, and one of the most beautiful in the world. The opinion
of distinguished architects is that from their standpoint it is the
most perfect building constructed in the last two centuries.—*
Capitol Tour Guide, 1917.

In 1956 the 34,000th person to tour the Capitol that year, a
twelve-year-old boy from Milwaukee, was presented with a
scroll and a box of Wisconsin cheese.

In 1957, the governor initiated the Capitol Hostess Plan,
whereby "pleasant and attractive" young women were stationed at a booth in the rotunda. They provided summer
tourism information and served samples of Wisconsin cheese
as each group of visitors set out on a guided tour of the building.

On a scale of ten, put down eleven.—State Capitol junkie, rating
Wisconsin's.

A great outburst of patriotic sentiment marked the Lincoln
centenary in February 1909. The event was notable as the first
public gathering in the new Assembly chamber. Someone read
the Gettysburg Address, and pupils of Lincoln School gave the
flag salute. Probably the first nonlegislative use of the Assembly
chamber occurred the same week, a lecture by prohibitionist
Florence Richards of the Women's Christian Temperance
Union.

Liberty Loan drives were held in the Assembly chamber in 1918 to support the World War I effort. State officials gave patriotic speeches, and state employees pledged to subscribe to the loan. Employees also met in the rotunda at 8:15 each morning to spend fifteen minutes singing patriotic songs, under the leadership of the state law librarian. The walls echoed with "America," "Battle Hymn of the Republic," and "Keep the Home Fires Burning."

The Capitol Mutual Club was a cooperative enterprise for state employees that existed for many years. It operated a restaurant in the basement of the Capitol, arranged for hundreds of gifts for children whose Christmas "is not all that it should be," held picnics and Halloween parties, and generally offered association and companionship. Any member of the club who was taken ill was sent flowers and visited by a committee.

A barber shop operated in the basement of the Capitol in the 1920s. A circular room, it had marble walls, floors, and ceilings, five chairs, and showers and bathtubs in the back room. Later it moved across the street to the Park hotel and returned to the Capitol for a few more years beginning in 1961. In 1969 it was transformed into an ice cream parlor.

The murals in Wisconsin's Capitol recall a prewar era only dimly remembered today. In dreamy scenes, strong heroes and blue-eyed youths and maidens carry unfurling flags through a lilac haze. There is no state capitol that could be more appropriately adorned by these idyllic vignettes than this monument built by the Progressives.—Hitchcock and Seale, *State Capitols of the U.S.A.* (1976).

The funeral of Robert M. La Follette Sr.—U.S. Senator, Presidential candidate, and Governor of Wisconsin from 1901 to 1906—was held in the Capitol on June 22, 1925. The previous day, an estimated 40,000 persons paid their respects when the body lay in state in the rotunda. The line of people outside the Capitol extended completely around the Square. Once inside, they filed past the body in two columns from 11 A.M. to 7:30 P.M. "It was as simple a funeral as ever was," his son Philip wrote later, "the only thing different were the thousands of people."

Funerals that took place in the Capitol in later years included those of U.S. Senator Robert M. La Follette Jr., in 1953; three-term governor Philip Fox La Follette, in 1965; Governor-elect Orland Loomis, who died one month after being elected, in 1942; and University of Wisconsin President Glenn Frank Sr. and son Glenn Jr., who were killed in an automobile crash during Frank Sr.'s campaign for the U.S. Senate in 1940.

The funeral of Robert M. La Follette Jr. in February 1953.

After his rigorous campaign as an independent candidate for President in 1924, former governor (1901–1906) and Senator Robert Marion La Follette, Sr. (second from right) returned home to Madison. Hundreds of supporters greeted him at the Northwestern railroad station and accompanied him to the Capitol, where he spoke briefly on the south steps. Here he listens to election night returns in the governor's conference room, along with (l. to r.) Isen La Follette (wife of Philip), Anna Blaine (wife of John), son Philip, Governor John J. Blaine, and son Robert M. Jr. (Belle Case La Follette had stayed in Washington.) Wisconsin voted for La Follette but the rest of the country elected Calvin Coolidge. Less than eight months later, La Follette died in Washington, was mourned at the Capitol, and buried in Madison.

By 1969 protests were becoming commonplace as farmers, migrant workers, and citizens protesting foreign policy arrived regularly to speak their piece. One time hundreds of people swarmed through the Capitol and occupied the Assembly chamber to protest welfare cutbacks.

Made nervous by bomb threats and antiwar demonstrations at the university, the Capitol closed its doors, posted national guardsmen outside, and screened visitors. Extra security officers—enough to protect a small city—were hired and trained in crash courses. Instead of one gun for the entire force as before, each officer carried a gun. (There was even thought given to having flocks of geese patrol the corridors, as in Scotland, where they are trained to honk loudly if visitors get too close to the crates of Scotch.)

Demonstrators carried on outside the Capitol but never entered the building. The Capitol survived a decade of unrest virtually unscarred.

Several hundred demonstrators protesting state investments in South Africa spread their sleeping bags on the marble floor and camped in the rotunda for fifteen days in 1985. Described as "exceedingly polite," they played cards and dominoes and danced. Leaders coordinated operations from a small office provided by a gracious governor.

In recent years champions of various causes have offered novel sights:
• The pastoral: On the Capitol grounds, an encampment of cows, bales of hay, and farmers unhappy about a proposed interstate highway.
• The absurd: Lining the rotunda, a row of environment-friendly chemical toilets for vacation homes.
• The incongruous: In the Assembly parlor, grimy laundry displayed by opponents of a state ban on phosphates in laundry detergents.

Crowds were silent and orderly at the chilling sight of a Ku Klux Klan parade around Capitol Square in October 1924. An estimated 1,300 persons in white sheets and hoods marched, while at least 500 others occupied flag-bedecked autos bringing up the rear. Marchers walked four abreast with their arms folded across their chests.

Farmers and cows with bales of hay camped on the Capitol grounds in 1976 to protest a proposed interstate highway that would remove many acres of land from production and divide up farms.

As early as 1916 community celebrations took place at the Capitol at Christmastime. The Rotary Club arranged for a forty-foot tree to be erected at the King Street entrance and for a smaller tree under the dome. On Christmas Eve, the Madison Military Band and the A Cappella Choir performed traditional music. The concert demonstrated the acoustical shortcomings of the Capitol, and the *Wisconsin State Journal* complained that the voices were barely audible because of the "scraping of feet and motley conversations" of the crowd of 2,500. In 1923 a transplanted music teacher from the Hawaiian Islands developed the idea of holding a nativity pageant, which became an annual event. High school music groups stationed around the upper levels of the rotunda respond when trumpeter-angels step up to the railing high overhead in the dome to herald the holiday season.

In recent years a Menorah has been placed on the first floor of the rotunda and lighted in celebration of Hanukkah.

The Freedom from Religion Foundation in turn held its first Freethought Concert in 1987 to protest religious activities and symbols in the Capitol. "It's a healthy sign for Wisconsin," said an observer, "that people can sing 'You Can't Win with Original Sin' against the backdrop of a Christmas tree." Also on the song list were "Frosty the Snowman" and "I'm Your Friendly Neighborhood Atheist."

A day or two before Thanksgiving a flat-bed truck arrives from the northern part of the state with a forty-foot holiday tree. It takes about twenty people to steer a fifteen-foot-wide tree through the doorway and into the rotunda. The stand is attached to the tree before it is raised upright with a system of wires and pulleys.

Scaffolding is erected so that the tree can be decorated with 1,800 multicolored lights and 3,000 snowflakes crocheted by senior citizens.

The forty-foot holiday tree reaches the second floor of the Capitol.

Controversies and Sore Losers

A plan proposed in 1907 would have extended Capitol Park all the way to Lake Monona. Professor John Olin, a promoter of parks for Madison, saw it as "a proper setting for the new capitol which would make a picture for future generations to cause a thrill of pride in every Wisconsin heart." Landscape architect John Nolen developed the concept into a Grand Mall 400 feet wide and 1,000 feet long flanked by government buildings and culminating with a theater and resort hotel on the lake. To some, the combination of this magnificent park and the new Capitol would make Madison famous throughout the civilized world. To others, it was a wild scheme promoted by those who stood to benefit from enhanced property values. After weeks of heated debate, Capitol Park stayed the way it was.

The new state house will in time, probably in less than a century, be torn down and supplanted by another and larger capitol, but during all the years the seat of government will remain unchanged and unchangeable. Therefore the wisdom, the

A forty-five-foot high retaining wall stands where John Olin's dream for Madison would have been: a park and grand boulevard connecting the Capitol and Lake Monona. Eighty years later, illusionist artist Richard Haas approached the fulfillment of Olin's plan by transforming the wall into an Italianate terrace that offers a view of the Capitol, Madison lakes, and a grotto in the bargain. Another unrealized vision for this site is alluded to elsewhere in the mural, the auditorium and convention center designed by Frank Lloyd Wright.

desirability, the necessity of providing now for fitting sur-roundings for the capitol.—Milwaukee Journal, March 2, 1907.

The Capitol was fully occupied as soon as it was finished, and within a few years working conditions were described as deplorable. "The cramped quarters of departments," wrote the *State Journal* in 1929, "have brought about unwholesome conditions for employees whose work is carried on under grave difficulties in basement corners and the ends of halls, with a varying temperature endangering health, and a cry of 'Move On.'" One of the most unusual arrangements had the statistical department of the railroad commission occupying a women's restroom.

Why, God bless you, there is not a practical man upon the committee or upon the Commission. . . . What do the people of the state of Wisconsin want of such an expensive and large Capitol building? The Assembly will not increase in twenty years. The Senate will remain the same. The Supreme Court will not need more judges. The bureaus of the state will not grow ten per cent in any of the departments in twenty years. Then why such a Capitol building? There is no call for it except from those who want to build a monument to their stupidity in burdening the people of the state with a high tax for years to come.—Senator J. J. McGillvray, February 23, 1905.

In 1967 the governor's wife, who considered the governor's reception room dismal, revealed plans to paint the walls off-white, take up the carpets, and change the drapes. The elaborate room had been painstakingly designed in Venetian

Renaissance style in imitation of the Doge's palace. Her news alarmed preservationists and prompted the legislature to pass a bill setting up a State Capitol and Executive Residence Board to review any such proposed departures from the original design of the Capitol and to defend its integrity if necessary. The committee met—three decorators, two architects, three senators, three assemblymen, and the governor's wife—and approved the decorating plans.

Women were not part of the Capitol scene until well after 1948, when this picture of lobbyists and others interested in a particular bill was taken in the Senate parlor. The first women to serve in the Assembly were elected in 1924: Mildred Barber of Marathon County, Hellen M. Brooks representing Green Lake and Waushara counties, and Helen Thompson of Price County, who campaigned on "no promises, no slogans, no platform. I'm going to proceed cautiously and hear the pro's and con's before I cast my vote." Only Thompson was reelected in 1926.

The first woman elected to the Senate was Kathryn Morrison of Platteville, in 1974. The first woman to serve on the Supreme Court was Shirley S. Abrahamson, appointed in 1976 and elected in 1979 and 1989.

The scramble for furniture and office space in the Capitol inspires desperate action. An assemblyman who had lost his large walnut desk along with a committee chairmanship dramatized his distress by creating a desk out of four orange crates and two wooden planks. The secretary of state threatened to chain himself to his desk to protect the conversion of his offices into eight legislative offices. He moved out but retains a ground floor cubbyhole office to fulfill the requirement in the state constitution that the secretary of state have an office in the Capitol. The state treasurer simply ignored an order to quit the Capitol for one of the new state office buildings. "In the old days," one official recalled, "only legislative leaders had offices. Most legislators operated out of their pockets. Some were hard-pressed to find a place to hang their coat."

If someone doesn't draw the line somewhere, we may one day find the governor himself relegated to a sterile suite in one of the faceless state monoliths down the road and the Supreme Court meeting in a Holiday Inn.—Editorial, *Capital Times*, July 25, 1980.

In 1975 the state adopted a policy to prevent retiring legislators who had become sentimentally attached to their office furniture from purchasing it at bargain prices and carting it home, even if their successors did prefer modern steel and plastic furniture. Too many leather chairs and rolltop desks were leaving the Capitol at ridiculously low prices, said a Senate committee. Much original furniture is still missing, and the restoration team remains on the lookout for pieces that got away.

Political demonstrations and bomb threats in 1970 prompted a proposal for covering the Capitol's windows. Many considered such self-defense measures to be futile and dreaded creating the appearance of an armed fortress. One senator, who was looking forward "to spring and the sounds and sweet smells of the awakening earth," wondered rhetorically whether "we'll suffer here in stifling heat behind windows that won't open?" Facing up to its "distasteful responsibility," the state went ahead and installed shatter-proof plastic shields over ground floor and first floor windows.

I notice that our ship of state, the visible and material part of it which costs millions of dollars, in the capitol park has three masts and when completed will have four. If I built a building costing that much money, I certainly would not put unsightly poles up on it. No one seems to have the gumption or the nerve to call attention to this, but I want to enter my protest against such an exhibition of bad taste. If I were in a country town or on a country road I would not be surprised to see a flagpole on a barn or a tobacco shed, but not on a million dollar building. Will some of the residents of this city or state kindly look up at these and then give me a reason why they should remain there?—Letter to the Editor, *Wisconsin State Journal,* June 14, 1914.

A particularly bad solution to the eternal problem of parking was proposed in 1969. Assembly Bill 111 would have permitted cars to park along the pedestrian walkways that lead up to and encircle the building. Envisioning a sea of parked cars on the Capitol lawn and oil stains on the pavement, legislators said No.

Dear Sir: We are sending you tonight under separate cover, six copies of the design of the cuspidors.—George Post to Lew Porter, November 24, 1911.

Poets Corner

Cuspidors usually don't inspire poetry, but the ones that served users of chewing tobacco and decorated Capitol hallways and stairways for many years have been so immortalized. It all began in 1955 when the state announced that it had 167 brass cuspidors that had outlived their usefulness and would be offered for sale to state legislators and officials for ten dollars each. Collectors and constituents were soon begging their state representatives for one of the fancy cuspidors, which weighed 40 pounds and bore the state seal. The poetic request proved most effective for a woman from Waterford who prevailed upon her state senator in verse.

I can picture it so clearly
In the hallway near the door;
A prize that we hold dearly,
A big brass cuspidor.

It's a friendly personality,
And every day it tends
To beam with informality
In welcoming our friends.

It's becoming an obsession
This picture that I see,
That brass in my possession,
Would curb this tensity.

Perhaps some law promoter
Would read this so-called poem,
And help this troubled voter
To make our house a home.

For this ornamental treasure
In our home, you must agree,
Would be loved beyond measure,
By a grateful family.

The Governor's office in 1916. On the floor is one of the coveted cuspidors.

Already bombarded by requests for cuspidors, the senator
replied:

> *I read with deep sincerity*
> *That you're in a muddled hash;*
> *'Twould signify prosperity*
> *To own this thing of brass.*
>
> *Alas, alack, you're not alone*
> *To covet such a prize*
> *For many and more would seek to own*
> *A "handy" thing this size.*
>
> *Though I'd like to share this treasure,*
> *So sorry it can't be done,*
> *We must deprive you of the pleasure,*
> *For we're limited to one.*

After reading the exchange of verse in the newspapers,
Governor Walter J. Kohler Jr. gallantly shipped to the woman
his cuspidor and this poem:

> *Some women want a new mink coat*
> *Others three or four,*
> *But you're the one that gets my vote;*
> *You want a cuspidor.*
>
> *I surely did appreciate*
> *Your clever poetry.*
> *That's why you'll get by freight*
> *The one they saved for me.*
>
> *This lovely forty pounds of brass*
> *Which I had planned to treasure,*

Now goes to you, because, my lass,
'Twill give you much more pleasure.

For every lucky new cuspidor owner there were three or four disappointed bidders. The proud owners converted the historic cuspidors (university undergraduates used to work their way through school polishing them) into lamp bases, planters, and doorstops for homes and offices all over the state of Wisconsin. Finally the surplus division of the Bureau of Purchases circulated this announcement:

Alas, dear friends, this final note
From we old cuspidors
Which many of you had wished to tote
From the Capitol's corridors.

For years we stood so bright and clean
At stations here and there
If we were used, a smile was seen,
If not, a brassy glare.

But now, dear friends, our job is done,
It seems we're too old-fashioned
We're glad to know you've wanted one,
That's why we have been rationed.

We're sorry that we were so few
But we're not the human race.
So wish us all luck in our new
And final resting place.

P.S. If you haven't gathered by now,
they're all gone, there ain't no more.

The replica of the Liberty Bell that stands on the first floor of the south wing, just below the Senate chamber, was given to Wisconsin in about 1950 by the U.S. Treasury. It is one of fifty-three that were made in France for a World War II savings bond drive. In 1968 the bell began what was to be a tour of Wisconsin communities. Sheboygan was its first and only stop though. No other community, as it turned out, was particularly interested in having or quite knew what to do with the gigantic bell. Over the years Sheboygan became quite attached to the bell and officials objected strenuously to giving it back when the state took steps in 1975 to reclaim it for the Capitol in time for the Bicentennial celebration. Sheboygan visitors now say that its prominent position in the Capitol compensates for the void it left in Fountain Park.

An Abundance of Badgers

The Capitol is crawling with badgers, the official state animal. A twenty-four-karat-gold badger clings to the top of the statue on the dome. A stone badger is tucked into the left corner in the carving of the west pediment (at the sculptor's request, the Capitol Commission supplied a live badger for a model). A badger emerges from the pine forest in the mural behind the speaker's platform in the Assembly chamber. Elsewhere in the Capitol painted badgers inhabit the ceilings, and imposing stone half-badgers (often mistaken for toads, frogs, pigs, or rats) loom high above the entrances to the Supreme Court, the Senate, the Assembly, and the Hearing Room on the second floor. Hundreds of brass badgers appear in the state seal on the plates behind doorknobs.

The 1,200-pound bronze badger that stands guard outside the governor's office once sailed the seas to China and Japan. The badger was a gift from the U.S. government and was mounted on the pilot house of the first *U.S.S. Wisconsin*, commissioned in 1901. Around the time of World War I it was removed when the battleship was stripped down for business, and its whereabouts became unknown. In 1988 State Historical Society detectives discovered it had been decorating the superintendent's garden at the U.S. Naval Academy in Annapolis, Maryland, for the past 60 years. Many miles of red tape later, the badger is back home, though only on loan. Officially it remains U.S. government property.

A cat named Harriette, who used to roam the Capitol, disrupted a session of the senate one night in 1913 when she sailed through the senate gallery like a cyclone, meowing strenuously. With the debate suspended, a faint chorus of meows could be heard. Capitol police ripped away a portion of a new floor to reveal Harriette's family of kittens, imprisoned by carpenters who had been installing the floor earlier in the day.

Live animals are prohibited in the Capitol (except when accompanying the visually handicapped) but occasionally one slips in, such as the deer that appeared at the Capitol one fine spring day in 1989. She raced past Max Drexler's Bavarian Brass Band, which was playing a polka for the lunchtime crowd on the King Street walkway, jumped a three-foot cement wall, darted into the Capitol, skidded on the marble floor of the rotunda several times, then raced outdoors again. The doe was captured two blocks away and released several miles south of Madison.

A raccoon stopped by the Capitol one May day in 1961 without an appointment and called on members of the Assembly and the secretary of state, but no one was in. The raccoon first toured the Assembly, which was not in session. Guards and workmen chased it to an open window. It tumbled out the

The badger (*taxidea taxus*—how fitting, some say) has been closely associated with Wisconsin since territorial days when miners in southwestern Wisconsin, too busy digging for lead to build houses, lived in abandoned mine shafts and makeshift burrows—like badgers.

window, landed on the first floor balcony outside the secretary of state's office, and climbed through the Secretary's open window. Office workers shrieked and scattered. Guards reappeared and eventually caught the raccoon in a net and released it elsewhere.

When the squirrel population on the Capitol grounds reached 400 in 1987, state officials drew the line. Healthy squirrels were eating too many flower bulbs, and "squirrelly" squirrels (probably the result of inbreeding) presented threat of disease. Hinting broadly, the state stopped putting out squirrel feed and dismantled most of the squirrel houses. The squirrels got the message. The population is now about sixty.

Pigeons and bats frequent the Capitol building. They find its cracks and crevices make excellent nesting places, and its wide open spaces are great for swooping. One night seventeen bats soared through the Supreme Court corridors and conference room. From outdoors the Capitol looked like a haunted house. Another night more than thirty bats were caught in the Assembly chamber. The bats are captured with nets and released in Capitol Park.

In 1924 an army of cockroaches overran the Capitol, subsisting chiefly on the glue on stamps and in book covers and bindings. Letters that had been mailed came back because of the glueless stamps, and books took on a mottled effect because of the cochroaches' consumption of dye.

Shooting quail was popular sport in Capitol Park in the middle of the nineteenth century. "Hundreds of these lovable little creatures have been slain upon the village plat," the newspaper reported. A century later, even though pigeons were not regarded as lovable little creatures, the public disapproved of shooting them on the Capitol grounds. In the 1940s, one man had the job of controlling the pigeon population with his .22 rifle. He usually went out early in the morning, before people started coming to work, because women especially "give me the very dickens when they see me shooting."

The stuffed eagle that hovers over the speaker's chair in the Assembly is a likeness of Old Abe, a bald eagle from the Eau Claire area that took part in Civil War battles fought by the Eighth Wisconsin Regiment. Old Abe made his home in the Capitol until 1881, when he perished from fumes from a paint fire; Abe returned stuffed but he was finished off for good in the Capitol fire of 1904. Or shall we say *she?* Recent evidence would indicate that Old Abe was female. Her screaming battle cry suggested to one expert the fierce temper characteristic of a female eagle, and reports have surfaced that Old Abe laid eggs in later years. Such scandalous news was probably hushed up to spare the state and its soldiers the embarrassment of having had a *girl* mascot.

There was one loss that seems to me just now greater than any of the others—greater, some will think, than all others. I can hardly get my pencil to say that Old Abe, too, is gone. That grand old eagle has come to be everybody's bird. Of the thousands of visitors . . . there was not one in a hundred who did not know the "Wisconsin War Eagle" about as well as he

Eagles on the bronze lamps outside the Wisconsin Supreme Court have shiny beaks. Some attorneys rub them for good luck before entering the courtroom to argue their cases.

knew Old Abe, the great war president.—Wisconsin State Journal, February 24, 1904.

A 400-million-year-old starfish fossil can be seen in a marble stairway in the north wing. Experts believe the starfish to be Genus Palaester, dating back to the Paleozoic era, at which time it was living in a primeval sea bottom. The marble came from Tennessee. The fossil is located on the fourth step of the west staircase of the second floor grand stairway in the north wing. Geologists say fossils of starfish are extremely rare because they lack the rigid skeleton necessary for preservation as fossils. A fossil resembling a giant snail appears in the wall of the Hearing Room in the north wing.

Chronology

1829 Federal district judge James Doty falls in love with and buys 1,200 acres of swampy but beautifully situated land between two lakes, names it after President James Madison.

1836 Territorial legislature meets from October to December in two-story frame building in Belmont to draft a constitution; Doty lobbies successfully for capital at Madison.

1837 Thirty-six workmen arrive from Milwaukee by ox team to start work on first capitol on isthmus site; with appropriate ceremony, cornerstone is laid, July 4; piecemeal construction—red brick, tin dome—drags on for years.

1837 Legislature meets in Burlington, now in the state of Iowa, from November 6 until December 13 when fire destroys temporary capitol.

1838 Legislature meets for first time in Madison in first capitol, where hogs snuffle in basement and ink freezes in inkwells.

1857 Legislature provides for new, enlarged capitol.

1869 Dome (last and most satisfactory portion of the structure) of second Madison capitol completed.

1882 Legislature approves enlarging the capitol with construction of two traverse wings, north and south.

1883 Eight workmen die when south wing collapses during construction, November 8.

1904 Capitol largely destroyed by fire, February 27.

1905 Agitation for moving capital from Madison to either Oshkosh or Milwaukee is put to rest by preliminary appropriations for new capitol; thousands of feet of rope, laid down to mark outline of proposed capitol, stolen overnight.

1906 Capitol Commission selects architectural firm of George B. Post & Sons; construction begins with west wing, October 12.

1907 Legislature appropriates $6 million for new capitol; first shipment of granite arrives, August 11.

1908 East wing construction begins.

1909 Legislature convenes with temporary furniture in not-quite-finished west wing, January 13; stonecutter dies when 300 tons of granite fall from west pediment, October 24.

1910 East wing is completed; construction of dome and south wing begins.

1911 Supreme Court moves into east wing in January; construction begins on rotunda and dome; John Nolen designs landscaping.

1911 Governor orders state to furnish uniforms for Capitol police to improve public image.

1913 Senate moves into chambers in south wing; dome painting arrives in Madison in June; architect George B. Post, active to the end, dies in New York on November 28.

1913–14 Panama Canal opens at same time artist completes Senate mural showing wedding of East and West.

1914 North wing construction begins; *Wisconsin* statue is hoisted into place, July 20; dome painting fixed in place in October.

1915 Rotunda and dome are completed; "unusually successful" murals, "inasmuch as they harmonize to an extraordinary degree with the color scheme," placed in Supreme Court in June; guided tours begin.

1916 University of Wisconsin Junior Prom held in rotunda (canvas partition shuts off unfinished north wing from dance floor), basement restaurant used for the first time, dancing amid Oriental splendor till 4 A.M. February 12; Madison Military Band, A Cappella Choir, and trumpet quartet provide music for Christmas Eve program in rotunda.

1917 With completion of north wing, Capitol is essentially finished; Capitol Commission is terminated and its functions transferred to state Department of Engineering; first guidebook is published; world's first electric voting machine installed in Assembly.

1918 Lew Porter, secretary of Capitol Commission and supervising architect, dies in Madison on April 16.

1921 Newly installed floodlights illumine outer dome, December 24.

1922 Gold star flowerbed dedicated.

1925 Funeral of Senator Robert M. La Follette Sr., "Wisconsin's most beloved and illustrious son," in rotunda June 21.

1926 Statue of Civil War hero Hans Christian Heg unveiled by boyhood friend, October 17.

1927 Charles A. Lindbergh circles dome three times before landing in Madison for speaking engagement, August 22.

1929 Basement restaurant closes.

1931 First radio broadcast of an inauguration from the Capitol when Governor Philip F. La Follette is sworn in.

1931 Tours to top of the outer dome discontinued as officials fear for safety of crowds of people making the climb.

1939 WPA workers install Capitol Park sprinkler system; new voting machine and first sound system installed in Assembly.

1943 Air raid warning program begun.

1948 Wisconsin Centennial celebration begins at Capitol, January 5; U.W. Junior Prom returns to Capitol after twenty years on campus, hundreds of white balloons released from dome as Lawrence Welk Orchestra plays "I'll Dance at Your Wedding," February 6; twelve-mile-long parade on Capitol Square for Statehood Day, May 29.

1948 Switchover to dial phone system in December, eliminating need for "Number, please?" operators.

1957 *Wisconsin* statue washed, wire-brushed, primed, and gold-leafed, July.

1959 Automatic elevators replace cage-type passenger elevators and displace elevator operators.

1961 Capitol barber shop reopens (closes in 1963).

1964 Art Fair held on Capitol grounds for the first time.

1965 Electrical system converted from direct current (DC) to alternating current (AC); Capitol dedicated for the first time, July 7.

1968 Cherrywood paneling in governor's conference room painted white; State Capitol and Executive Residence Board established to monitor plans for future alterations.

1969 Father James Groppi and demonstrators protesting budget cuts for welfare occupy Assembly chamber for eleven hours, and case involving contempt charge travels to U.S. Supreme Court, which rules for Groppi.

1971 Anti-firebomb plastic shields installed over windows against Vietnam-era demonstrations.

1973 Capitol cleans house, sells off original furniture and accessories at "garage sale."

1977 Senate restroom subdivided to accommodate first women senators.

1980 Landscape architect hired to sort out problems, design and coordinate plans for Capitol Park.

1980 Wiring repaired and pedestal beneath *Wisconsin* statue is lighted for first time in twelve years.

1982 State Building Commission approves $1 million plan to restore 638 windows; Governor and staff move out of Capitol during restoration of executive offices; Professional Grounds Management Society awards Wisconsin Capitol grand prize.

1984 Wednesday night outdoor Concerts on the Square series inaugurated, June 27.

1986 Anti-apartheid demonstrators use wood, cardboard, and old doors to build a nine-shack shantytown in Capitol Park symbolizing housing conditions in South Africa.

1987 *A Vision Shaped in Stone: Wisconsin's Capitol* film is produced for Wisconsin Public Television.

1988 Circuit court rules that nativity pageant and Menorah lighting ceremony in Capitol do not violate principle of separation of church and state as long as government officials do not participate.

1988 State Hygiene Laboratory determines that arsenic used to preserve stuffed eagle (Old Abe II) in Assembly chamber does not pose a health hazard.

1988 Presidential candidates Dole, Dukakis, Gore, Jackson, and Simon swing their campaigns through the Capitol.

1989 University scales back expansion plans for library that would have obstructed view of Capitol from Bascom Hill.

1989 State Building Commission approves inclusion of air-conditioning in Capitol-improvement program.

1990 Civil War and Spanish American War artifacts and displays removed from Capitol with closing of Grand Army of the Republic Museum on fourth floor.

1990 Smoking prohibited in public areas.

1990 *Wisconsin* statue restored and regilded for third time.

1991 Publication of 33d edition of *Official Guide and History*, 64 pages; publication of coloring book and guide to the history, conservation and regilding of *Wisconsin*.

Startling Statistics

MEASUREMENTS (in feet)
Height of Capitol (to top of statue):   284.4
To observation deck (last stop for visitors):   105.4
Height of dome statue: 15.5
Length of Capitol, north to south or east to west: 438.8
Breadth of each wing: 125
One side of Capitol Park: 764.7
Length of tunnel between Capitol
   and power plant: 2,403
Diameter of dome mural: 34
Height of figures in dome mural: 13

EQUIVALENTS
Height of Capitol in stories: 24
Number of sides of Capitol Park per mile: 7
Number of laps around Capitol Park per four miles: 7
Cubic space (in cubic feet):   7,656,842
Gross square feet: 448,300
Percentage of space assignable: 33

Capitol Park, in acres: 13.4

Grounds, in acres: 7

Sidewalks and driveways, in acres: 3.5

PRICETAGS

To construct building: $5,210,976

With extras

  (art, furniture, power plant, etc.): $7,203,826

Amount insured for today: $160,000,000

Amount paid in property taxes: $0

Cost to clean exterior in 1965: $41,000

Cost of *Wisconsin* statue on dome: $20,325

To gild *Wisconsin* in 1914: $325

To regild *Wisconsin* in 1932: $444

In 1957: $1,100

In 1990: $95,000

Rotunda mosaics: $21,250

Senate murals: $12,000

Supreme Court murals: $28,000

Governor's Conference Room murals: $25,000

Nine pieces of French walnut furniture

  in Governor's Conference Room: $4,081

Bronze cuspidors: $3,600

Flagpoles: $413

Brass "Wisconsin" doorknob in 1983: $72

Brass plate behind doorknob: $183

Overtime parking ticket on Capitol Square: $5

Rank of "How much did the Capitol cost?"

  among questions asked of tour guides: 1

GRAND TOTALS

Rooms: 700
Windows: 638
Light fixtures: 10,000
Fireplaces: 5
Working fireplaces: 1
Pieces of painted glass in rotunda mosaics: 400,000
Eagles on bronze lamps on second floor bridges: 160

ENTHUSIASMS AND EXCESSES

Number of persons known to have stood on *Wisconsin's*
    head and waved American flag: 1
Number of years that Margaret Rupp Cooper was harpist
    for nativity pageant: 56
Number of years Earl Peterson changed the lightbulbs
    in the Capitol: 23
Number of people who visit Capitol Park
    each year: 700,000
Who test their constitutional rights at the Great Midwest
    Marijuana Harvest Festival every fall: 5,000
Number of people who took tour of building
    in 1990:   70,463
Who took tour in May 1990:   17,727
Rank of Peanut M&M's among snack items sold
    in basement vending machines: 1
Number of Q-tips used to clean Assembly murals
    in 1989:   20,000
Number of sheets of gold to refurbish
    Wisconsin statue: 12,800
Size in square feet of largest Assembly mural: 675
Tons of steel in the dome: 2,500
Tons of cheese Governor Julius P. Heil (1939–43)
    sent out at Christmastime: 9

Of the 900 men in Hans Christian Heg's regiment,
number named Ole: 126
Distance in miles governor's doorknob traveled aboard
space shuttle *Discovery:*   3,000,000
Number of Cokes served at 1948 Prom: 7,200
Rank of mittens and gloves of all items
in Lost & Found: 1

INHABITANTS

Building employees: 1,600
Assembly members: 99
Their average age: 47
Youngest: 32
Female assembly members in 1991:   31
Female assembly members in 1941:   1
Senators: 33
Their average age: 45
Youngest: 27
Female senators in 1991:   4
Female senators in 1941:   0
Supreme Court justices: 7
Their average age: 64
Youngest: 50
Female justices: 1
Governors to serve in this capitol: 22
Number born in Wisconsin: 20
Age of Governor Walter ("Woof Woof") Goodland
when he took office in 1943:   80
His collar size: 22
Age of Governor Philip F. La Follette
when he took office in 1931:   33
Number of governors whose father also had been
governor: 2
Number of Indian Sikhs who have been tour guides: 1

HOLIDAYS, HEARTS, AND FLOWERS

Lights on the holiday tree: 1,800
Crocheted snowflakes on the holiday tree: 2,500
Weddings performed in 1990:   52
Governors who never married: 1
Flower beds: 31
Flower varieties: 60
Tulips: 46,000
Alternanthera plants needed to spell out
   AMERICA'S DAIRYLAND: 12,000
Basil plants in gold star bed: 800
Rose pink hibiscus trees on King Street walkway: 6
Trees in Capitol Park: 158
Elms lost to Dutch elm disease: 42
Elms remaining: 3
Days to mow the lawn: 2

Photo Credits

p. 2 State Historical Society of Wisconsin WHi(X3)2696; p. 4 State Historical Society of Wisconsin WHi(X32)5237; p. 7 photos lent by Martha Kilgour; p. 10 State Historical Society of Wisconsin WHi(X3)2062; p. 12 State Historical Society of Wisconsin WHi(X3)29044; p. 17 State Historical Society of Wisconsin, Kilgour Collection, WHi(X3)26494; p. 19 Wisconsin State Journal photo by [kids' eye view]; p. 25 State Historical Society of Wisconsin WHi(X3)11515; p. 27 James T. Potter, AIA; p. 31 DeLyle P. Runge, University of Wisconsin–Madison Archives #X252363; p. 37 State Historical Society of Wisconsin WHi(X3)12712; p. 41 Wisconsin State Journal photo by A. Craig Benson; p. 44 Wisconsin Tourism Development; p. 46 Wisconsin Department of Administration, Division of Buildings and Grounds; p. 49 photo lent by Betty L. Sauer; p. 52 L. Roger Turner; p. 58 Sally Benforado; p. 60 Sally Benforado; p. 63 photo hoax contrived by Cedric Parker, Capital Times; p. 64 Wisconsin Tourism Development; p. 67 Milwaukee Sentinel photo, State Historical Society of Wisconsin, WHi(X3)46146; pp. 68–69; Photoart House, State Historical Society of Wisconsin, WHi(X3)46145; p. 71 Capital Times photo by David Sandell; p. 74 United Press International Newspictures, State Historical Society of Wisconsin, WHi(X3)46147; p. 75 State Historical Society of Wisconsin, WHi(X3)18807; p. 77 Wisconsin State Journal photo by Craig Benson; p. 79 Wisconsin State Journal photo by [christmas tree]; p. 81 Mary Langenfeld, University of Wisconsin–Madison Archives #X252362; p. 83 State Historical Society of Wisconsin, WHi(X3)8844; p. 87 Meuer Photoart Collection, State Historical Society of Wisconsin, WHi(X22)20525; p. 93 Sally Benforado; p. 96 Sally Benforado.